Your Pony Your Horse

A Kid's Guide to Care and Enjoyment

CHERRY HILL

STOREY
BOOKS

Acknowledgments

Thanks to the following for their help with this manuscript:
Sally George
Richard Klimesh

The mission of Storey Publishing is to serve our customers by publishing practical information that encourages personal independence in harmony with the environment.

Edited by Lorin Driggs
Cover and text design by Carol J. Jessop, Black Trout Design
Cover photograph by Cherry Hill
Cover production by Susan Bernier
Text production by Wanda Harper Joyce and Susan Bernier
Photographs by Cherry Hill and Richard Klimesh, unless noted otherwise
Line drawings by Elayne Sears, unless noted otherwise
Indexed by Northwind Editorial Services

The information in this book is true and complete to the best of our knowledge. All recommendations are made without guarantee on the part of the author or Storey Publishing. The author and publisher disclaim any liability in connection with the use of this information. For additional information, please contact Storey Publishing, 210 MASS MoCA Way, North Adams, MA 01247.

Storey books are available for special premium and promotional uses and for customized editions. For further information, please call 1-800-793-9396.

Printed in the United States by Capital City Press
20 19 18 17 16 15 14 13 12 11

Library of Congress Cataloging-in-Publication Data
Hill, Cherry, 1947–
    Your pony, your horse : a kid's guide to care and enjoyment / Cherry Hill.
      p.   cm.
    "A Storey Publishing book."
    Includes bibliographical references (p.   ) and index. Summary: Introduces routines for handling and caring for a pony or horse, providing step-by-step instructions and discussing safety, responsibility, horse clubs, and other community activities.
    ISBN 0-88266-908-7 (pbk.)
    1. Horses—Juvenile literature.   2. Horsemanship—Juvenile literature.   3. Ponies—Juvenile literature. [1. Horsemanship. 2. Horses. 3. Ponies.] I. Title.
SF302.H54   1995
636.1—dc20
                                                   95-18319
                                                     CIP
                                                     AC

A PONY'S DREAM

by Cherry Hill

I'm walking through a meadow
The grass is green and tall
I plan on grazing all day long
But hear a friendly call.

"Diamond, Diamond, come to me"
The voice sounds by the gate
"You'd better stop your munching
We have to watch your weight."

My human friend then halters me
And leads me to my stall
I get a thorough grooming
While tied safely to the wall.

My hooves are cleaned of mud and stones
My chest and belly brushed
My mane and tail are fingered through
The grooming is not rushed.

Next a saddle and a pad
Are placed upon my back
We're getting ready for a ride
With safe and tidy tack.

We start out rather slowly
So my muscles can warm up
By the time we're out an hour
I'm frisky as a pup.

We take our time when walking home
I sigh and stretch my back
The trail ride felt good to me
I like my fitted tack.

Again I'm groomed and cared for well
My every need is met
It's when I'm hugged around my neck
My human's eyes get wet.

Am I dreaming or is this real?
Are **you** my human friend?
You are?! That's great! A dream come true.
May our friendship never end.

Dedication

To Rachael and Tyler
and other responsible, dedicated horse kids.
And to Matthew and Elizabeth.

Other Books by Cherry Hill

Horsekeeping on a Small Acreage

Becoming an Effective Rider

From the Center of the Ring

101 Arena Exercises

The Formative Years

Making Not Breaking

Maximum Hoof Power

Horse for Sale

Contents

Introduction

A Special Note to My Readers

I'm so excited for you! I think that horses are the most wonderful interest you could possibly have! Horses have given me so much enjoyment that I have spent my whole life learning about them. Now I'd like to help teach you how to care for your pony or your horse. This book and the other books I will recommend along the way are great sources of information about horses. But in order to become a really accomplished horse-person, you also need two special mentors.

What is a mentor? A mentor is a wise and dedicated teacher. One of the mentors you need to find is a person who has had a lot of positive experiences with horses and loves and respects them, someone who works safely with horses and can describe to you how and why you should do things a certain way. This person could be old or fairly young. He or she could be a professional horse trainer or riding instructor, your next-door neighbor, the man who works at the feed store, or your 4-H or Pony Club leader.

If you find a mentor who is willing to share knowledge with you and teach you about horses, you are **very lucky**. Do everything you can do to show your mentor that you are serious and want to learn. Pay attention when he or she is explaining something to you. Never arrive late or miss a scheduled meeting or lesson with your mentor. Be respectful and polite. A mentor is a very great treasure for you to find. Think of things you can do for your mentor to show your appreciation. Maybe you can offer to do something that will save her some time, like cleaning a few stalls for her or soaping and oiling some bridles.

The second mentor you need is a well-trained, trustworthy horse. In Chapter 2, I'll give you some specific advice on how to choose a horse that will be safe and fun for you to handle and ride. Keep in mind that you will learn most easily on a patient, well-trained, experienced horse that has already taught other young people how to ride. Usually such a horse will be old and wise but might not be the winner of a beauty contest. I've found that no matter what a horse looks like, if he is kind and safe and willing to teach you how to ride, you will love him dearly.

Horses can give you a lifetime of enjoyment.

A Note to Parents

There is something about the outside of a horse that is good for the inside of a child. I can remember as a preschooler that when I had the opportunity to groom and ride a horse, I did not want to wash my hands for fear of losing that wonderful smell. I encourage you to support your child's interest in horses.

The rest of my comments to you are going to sound like a bunch of do's and don'ts. They are! I hope you take my advice to heart so your child's experience will be safe and will add to the development of his or her character.

Most children who are 6 to 7 years old have the motor skills, confidence, and attention to safely learn to ride a horse. If you start your child too young, you could risk frightening him or her. Don't push your child into the show ring. Emphasize wholesome, safe fun before competition and teach your child that participating is winning.

Most good children's horses are between the ages of 8 and 20 or even older. *Geldings* are usually preferred because of their stable dispositions. It doesn't matter if a horse or pony is slightly arthritic as long as it is sound and has an exemplary temperament and very solid training and manners.

Gelding. A castrated male horse.

Horses are not people and should not be treated as people. They need to be treated as horses for their own well-being as well as your child's safety. Your child should be taught a sensitive but realistic approach to horses. The best way for a child to develop the proper attitude about horses is to first focus on responsible care for the horse.

Your child will need to learn many step-by-step routines for handling and caring for a pony or horse. Although this book will get your child started in the right direction, look for a high-quality instructor to regularly coach your child. The 4-H or Pony Club in your area may provide such instruction. Otherwise, you will have to look for a professional horse trainer or instructor who can help you with your child and pony or horse.

To find a good instructor for your child, ask your county Extension agent for several suggestions and a recommendation. If you know other children who are taking lessons, ask their parents how satisfied they are with the child's instruction program. Call several of the instructors that have been recommended to you and ask how long the instructor has been teaching, if he or she is certified, what style of riding is taught, the cost, and the length of lessons. If everything sounds acceptable, ask the instructor to provide you with two references. After you've checked the references, you should visit the facilities and view a lesson in progress before you entrust your child's safety to a particular instructor. The more time you spend selecting the best instructor for your child, the better your child's experience will be, and the fewer problems you will have. Become very familiar with the activity options for your child, and with the sources of more information listed in Chapter 8.

Through all phases of your child's equestrian development, he or she needs safe clothing and tack. You will need to invest in proper footwear and head-gear as well as other riding accessories. In addition, your child's horse or pony will require safe, suitable equipment for riding.

You might have heard the phrase "backyard horse-man." I hope you don't think that means you can keep a horse in your backyard! A small pony will need a minimum of an acre and carefully planned, safe facilities to live in.

I strongly encourage you to become very familiar with horse behavior. I've seen several instances where a parent **contributed** to an accident between a child and a horse because the parent panicked, did not know what to do and therefore either froze and did nothing, or did the wrong thing. Also, stay current on your first-aid knowledge and skills. They will come in handy for your child and friends as well as for their horses.

Being involved with horses requires an investment of time, money, and hard work. Depending on the age of your child, you may have to do a large share of the horsekeeping work yourself. I look on this as a bonus for you rather than a burden because caring for horses has given me so much enjoyment. You might find, as other parents have, that after you have cared for your child's horse for a while, you will want to get a horse of your own.

Realize that it will probably cost somewhere around $1500 per year or more to keep a horse. This figure represents routine costs such as feed, bedding, routine vet care, and *farrier* care.

Farrier. *A person who shoes horses.*

Be sure your child knows that he or she must make trade-offs in order to see that the horse is well cared for. Sometimes it will be necessary to miss a favorite TV program or a party to take care of a horse's special needs.

Avoid the *green* horse/green rider syndrome. Parents often think it would be nice to get a foal and let the child and young horse grow up together. However, this arrangement results in a greater chance for mistakes and mishaps. A child needs an older, well-trained, patient, and tolerant horse.

Note to readers. All italicized words are included in the glossary on page 141.

Consider carefully before deciding to teach your own child how to ride. Even if you are an experienced rider yourself, it is often better for the child to learn horse care, handling, and riding in a structured program. That's the beauty of being a member of an active youth group. You can participate by organizing meetings, fund-raisers, clinics, and shows and let your child benefit from the group's instructors. If you choose to enroll your child in private lessons with a certified instructor, choose your child's mentor carefully.

Be sure you read this book from cover to cover. You should know at least as much as your child does about horses. Refer to the recommended reading list on page 139 for other books that will provide more detailed information on various subjects: training, riding, health care, hoof care, facilities, management, safety, showing, and much more.

I am so grateful to my parents for encouraging me to pursue my interest in horses. Although I didn't **own** my first horse until I was 19, throughout my early childhood my parents created many opportunities for me to learn about horses and ride them. There are many ways you can help your child have a positive and very rewarding horse experience. I hope this book helps you and your young rider on the way.

Behavior

CHAPTER 1

How to Behave Around Horses

Horses are horses. They are not people. Although you might want to kiss your horse to show him how much you like him, he might think you are acting oddly and pull away suddenly. Or worse yet, he might nibble your lips to see if there is anything in them to eat and you could be hurt. Your horse will be the happiest when you do things that he understands. While he is learning more about you, you will learn more about what it is like to be a horse. For example, you will find that your horse appreciates a good scratch on the *withers* or the neck more than a pat on the nose.

    Just because you and your horse are buddies and you trust each other, don't be careless. You must always pay attention because just when you least expect it, your horse might suddenly jump sideways and smash your toes! Never fool around when you're near horses. I have seen children seriously hurt when they acted silly or pulled pranks involving horses. I don't want that to happen to you.

How Horses Behave

Here are some things I have learned about horses that will help you understand them and "speak their language."

Withers. *The part of the horse's spine where the neck joins the back.*

Horses Are Social Animals

Herd-bound. When a horse is too dependent on being near other horses. Also called barn sour when a horse doesn't want to leave the barn.

Horses like to be near other horses. Horses that live in herds may become *herd-bound*. When you try to remove one horse from the herd, all of the horses may become nervous and try to stay near the horse you are taking away. Or, the horse you are trying to take away might stop and refuse to leave the herd. To prevent this, you should not let horses get too attached to each other. A horse that is kept in his own pen or paddock and is handled regularly by you will think of **you** as his "herd-mate" and will look forward to your coming and spending time with him.

Pecking order. The order of dominance among horses in a herd.

If you have two or more horses together on pasture, one of them is the "top" horse in the pecking order. *Pecking order* is the rank of power or dominance in the herd. When you feed, the top horse will be the first one to get the food. That's why it is important to spread feed far apart so all horses will get some. Otherwise, the "bottom" horse might not get anything. Sometimes horses bite and kick each other to prove who is the top horse. You don't want to get between two horses that are deciding their pecking order or you might get hurt.

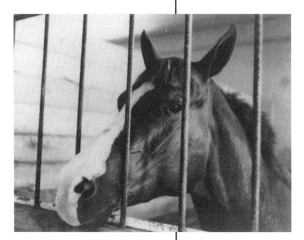

A confined horse can get bored and lonely. If you keep your horse in a stall or pen, he will depend on you to provide him with daily exercise.

Horses Are Wanderers

By nature, horses like to roam around and take a bite here and a bite there. This gives them exercise and allows them to eat while they are on the move. If you put your horse in a pen or a stall, you must provide him with feed and exercise every day because he can no longer roam and take care of those things himself.

If you confine your horse too long, he will become restless. When you finally do take him out, he might be hard to handle because he has so much energy to burn. How would you feel if you had to stay in your room for a whole week?!

Horses Would Rather Run than Fight

If your horse sees something he thinks is dangerous, he would rather run away from it than stand and fight. Your horse's ancestors survived for millions of years because of this. When a mountain lion approached a horse in ancient times, the horse did not stand there or try to defend himself against the sharp teeth and claws. The horse just broke into a gallop and tried to outrun the mountain lion. That's why some horses are so spooky and flighty. To them, a piece of blowing plastic or a huge rock might be an enemy in disguise. But even though a horse is afraid of something, his curiosity will usually get the better of him and he will try to figure out what the unfamiliar object is. It might take quite a long time, but in most cases the horse will eventually walk up to a suspicious object, smell it, and touch it with his nose.

Horses Have Keen Senses

Your horse uses his keen senses in many ways. For example, he keeps a watchful eye on everything around him and immediately notices when something changes. If your grooming bucket has been in one spot for weeks and you move it to the other side of the grooming area, watch your horse's reaction when you lead him into the barn. He might stop for a moment and get a look on his face that seems to say, "What the heck is going on here?!" He may even whistle and snort a little while he figures out that the bucket is OK in its new place. A horse's senses protect him and help him identify and locate things.

Smell

A horse uses his sense of smell to identify people, other horses, and things. Mares and foals bond to each other by their individual smells. Horses use smell along with vision to recognize objects and specific people. Your horse will learn to recognize your smell so that even in the dark, he could identify you.

Vision

Horses have better vision than you do in many ways. Horses are alert to even small changes around them. If a tiny squirrel moves in a tree quite a distance away, you might not see the squirrel, but your horse probably will. Also, your horse can see better at night than you can.

Sometimes a horse has a hard time focusing his eyes to get a clear picture of an object. He might have to raise or lower his head or tilt it a certain way to see things in certain positions. Horses have blind spots, places where they cannot see things unless they move their heads or bodies.

Whenever you are in a horse's blind spot, you must let him know you are there. Otherwise you might startle him and he might suddenly jump and hurt you. The best way to do this is to talk to the horse while you touch him: "Hi, Buck. I'm grooming your chest now."

Hearing

Your horse has better hearing than you do. His ears can detect sounds above and below the range of sounds your

A Horse's Blind Spots

- The area directly behind his tail

- The area of his back that lies directly behind his head

- The area directly in front of his forehead

- The area directly under his head on the ground and near his front legs

The dark areas indicate the horse's blind spots.

ears can hear, so he will hear small noises that you don't even notice. Sometimes a horse will jump when he hears a noisy truck or a high-pitched whistle — sounds that seem perfectly normal to you.

When a horse really wants to know what something is, he looks at it very hard, with his ears pointed toward the object. His ears act like funnels to catch even the faintest sound. Since horses have such good hearing, they can learn to distinguish your voice from other voices. And you don't have to talk loudly or scream at your horse. He can hear you just fine when you are speaking in a low or normal voice.

Touch

Your horse can easily feel a fly crawling around on the tips of the hairs on his belly. Because horses have such a sensitive sense of touch, you shouldn't use harsh *aids* on your horse. Often fingertip pressure or a slight weight shift is all that you need. Your horse's nose, lips, and other areas on his head are the most sensitive parts of his body, so you want to be very careful when handling them. Also whenever you use a bridle on a horse, you want to use light pressure with the reins.

Aid. An action from a rider or handler that tells a horse what to do.

Horses Can Be "A" Students

Horses have a great ability to learn what we want them to do when we use proper aids. It takes a good horse trainer to make a well-trained horse, but once a horse knows what he is supposed to do, he will remember it for a long time. Once a horse has learned that when you squeeze him with both legs he should trot, he will remember it for life. The horse's memory is almost as good as an elephant's!

Besides remembering good things, a horse also remembers bad habits. That's why you want to be sure your horse does not develop bad habits, because it will be very hard for you to get him to "forget" them.

Horses are copycats. If your horse sees another horse cross a creek, he will probably follow. But if your horse sees another horse balk and rear when asked to cross a creek, he might imitate that bad behavior.

Horse Talk

A horse communicates with his body, not words. Some of the most common examples of horse body language and what they mean are:

- Ears pinned back, head reaching toward you - "Stay back or I'll bite you."

- Ears forward, head high — "I wonder what that is over there?"

- Pawing with front feet — "I want to get out of here."

- Swishing tail (not at flies) — "I'm irritated" OR "My stomach hurts."

- Swinging his hindquarters toward you — "I'm

If you learn to "read" horse language, you will have a safer and more enjoyable time working with horses.

afraid" OR "I'm getting ready to kick you."

- Lifting or stomping one hind leg (not at flies) — "Warning: I might kick you" OR "I have a stomach-ache."

- Ears forward, head reaching toward you — "Hi, pal."

- Ears back toward you when you are riding — "I'm really concentrating and listening to you."

- Ears pinned back flat against the head — "I'm getting ready to buck."

Mares In Heat

Once a month during the spring, summer, and fall, when a mare is *in heat* or *in season,* she might have a period during which she is silly, grouchy, spooky, or even mean. If you have a mare that behaves this way when she is in heat, ask your veterinarian to examine her. There is a small chance that the vet might find that there is something wrong with the mare's reproductive system. Even if there is nothing wrong, it might be best to give your mare a few days off, without training or riding, every month when she is in heat.

Heat. *The part of a mare's reproductive cycle when she is ready to mate with a stallion.*

Choosing a Horse

Before you make the final decision about which particular horse to choose for your very own, you will need to consider many factors. These include the breed or type of pony or horse, its size, age, sex, level of training, temperament, color, and other qualities.

Pony or Horse?

Eohippus lived over 60 million years ago and was the ancestor of today's horses and ponies. Between then and now horses, classified as *Equus caballus,* have gone through many changes. Along the way, various *types* of horses evolved, which is why we have different breeds and types of horses and ponies today.

Horses are classified as heavy horses or light horses. Heavy horses are large horses used for farming and draft purposes. Light horses are those used for riding. Ponies are a subclassification of light horses. One of the main differences between a horse and a pony is that a pony is generally under 14•2 hands (58 inches) in height. A hand equals four inches. (See page 26 for how to measure your pony or horse.) Ponies are generally longer in their bodies than they are tall. Horses are generally over 14•2 in height. Horses are usually equal in body length and height.

Which Breed?

Breed. *A group of ponies or horses that have certain physical characteristics inherited from a common ancestor.*

A *breed* is a group of ponies or horses with common ancestors from which they have inherited certain physical characteristics, such as the size and shape of their heads and bodies, the way they move, and their color and markings. Ponies or horses that are the same breed usually resemble one another. That's what allows you to look at a particular horse and say, "That's an Arabian," or at a particular pony and say, "That's a Shetland."

Each breed has a *breed registry* that keeps track of all the members of the breed. To be registered as a member of a certain breed, a horse might need to pass an inspection to see if it has the physical characteristics of the breed.

Pony Breeds

Pony breeds vary in size, color, and gait.

BONNIE KREITLER

Shetland Pony

Driving. *Used to pull a cart or wagon.*

Shetland

Shetland is the smallest of ponies. The breed originated in the British Isles, but many are now bred in the United States. The American Shetland is mainly a fancy *driving* pony — a pony used to pull a cart. Shetlands can be almost any color, including multi-colored coat patterns similar to Paint Horses. Shetlands grow a very long coat in the winter, making them a good choice for cold climates. They are generally not noted for their smooth riding *gaits*. You might learn to ride on a well-trained Shetland Pony, but you would probably soon outgrow him.

Welsh

Welsh ponies originated in Wales, a part of Great Britain. They come in four sizes ranging from 12 to 15 hands. Three sizes are actual pony sizes (under 14•2 hands), while the larger Welsh size is referred to as a *cob* (small horse). A cob is often good for a rider who is too large for a normal-sized pony but not big enough yet for a large horse. You will see Welsh ponies in gray, *palomino,* and *roan.* They are considered to be excellent riding ponies.

Cob. *A small horse.*

POA

POA stands for Pony of the Americas, which is an American pony breed founded in 1956. The breed was developed by cross-breeding Shetland Ponies with Appaloosa Horses and a few Quarter Horses and Arabians (see following descriptions of these horses). POAs generally range in height from 11•2 to 13•2. They show a wide variety of coat patterns similar to those of Appaloosa Horses.

Connemara

Connemara is an Irish pony with influence from the Arabian breed. Generally one of the taller ponies, Connemaras range up to 14•2 hands. They are often gray or black but can be brown, *bay,* or *dun.* Connemaras are noted for very smooth gaits and make excellent riding ponies.

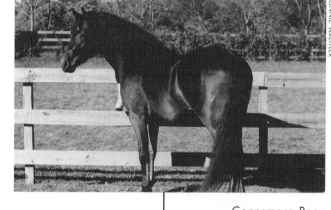

BONNIE KREITLER

Connemara Pony

Horse Breeds

Horse breeds vary in their size, body shape, color, and gaits.

American Saddlebred

Appaloosa

Morgan

American Saddlebred

The American Saddlebred is an American breed established in the 1800s in the southern United States for riding and driving. Today most Saddlebreds are of the show type with flashy gaits. *Height:* 16 hands.

Appaloosa

Appaloosa is a breed of spotted horses that originated in the north-western United States (Idaho, Oregon, Washington) in the land of the Nez Perce Indians. Appaloosas might be leopard (spots all over), have a white blanket over the hips with spots in the blanket, or be frosted all over. *Height:* 14•2 to 15•2 hands.

Arabian

The Arabian breed has had the greatest effect on all other breeds. The Arabian traces back to the year 786 in Arabia. The Arabian usually has a beautiful head, short back, floating action, and often a high tail carriage. (The endurance and pleasure type horses illustrated on page 21 are both Arabians.) The most common color for Arabians is gray. *Height:* 14•2 to 15 hands.

Morgan

The Morgan is an American breed that traces back to 1795 to a single stallion owned by a man named Justin Morgan. Morgans are good for driving and riding. The Morgan breed has had an influence on the development of the American Saddlebred breed. It is a compact horse with flashy gaits. *Height:* 14•1 to 15•2.

Paint

A Paint is a *stock* type horse (see page 22) with painted body color — large blocks of white and black or white and brown. Paint Horses usually have Quarter Horse and Thoroughbred ancestors. *Height:* 14•3 to 15•3.

Paint

Palomino

The Palomino Horse has a golden body color and a light to white mane and tail. A palomino color can occur in almost any breed, particularly Quarter Horses. *Height:* 14•1 to 16 hands.

Pinto

Pintos can be horses of almost any type (stock, pleasure, show) that have painted body color. Think about this one: all Paints can be registered as Pintos but not all Pintos can be registered as Paints. *Height:* 15 to 16 hands.

Quarter Horse

The Quarter Horse is the oldest and most popular American breed, having its beginning in the 1600s in the state of Virginia. The breed was developed for working and racing. The Quarter Horse breed is the basis for many other stock horse breeds such as the Paint, Appaloosa, and Palomino. *Height:* 15 hands to 15•3.

Quarter Horse

Draft horse. *A horse of one of the breeds of "heavy horses" developed for farm or freight work.*

This gelding is half Quarter Horse and half Selle Français so is not a registered horse. He is considered a part-bred or a grade horse. He is of the hunter or sports horse type.

Thoroughbred

The Thoroughbred is an English breed from the early 1700s which traces to three sires: the Byerly Turk, the Darley Arabian, and the Godolphin Arabian. It is a long, lean horse that can cover ground in long strides. *Height:* 15•2 to 16 hands.

Warmblood

This is a general term used to describe many European breeds of sport horses. The name Warmblood comes from a cross between a *hot blood horse* like an Arabian or Thoroughbred and a *cold blood horse* like a *draft horse.* What do you get? A Warmblood horse. In size, a Warmblood is somewhere between a Thoroughbred and a Draft horse. *Examples:* Dutch Warmblood, Selle Français, Trakehner, Hanoverian. *Height:* about 16 to 17 hands.

Grade

A grade horse is one that is not registered with a breed association. He might be a *purebred* without papers or he might be a *crossbred.*

To Capitalize or Not to Capitalize?

When a breed or color description is capitalized, it usually means the horse is registered with a specific breed organization. For example, when a horse is said to be a Paint Horse, he is probably registered with the American Paint Horse Association (APHA). The same would probably be true for the following: Palomino Horse (PHBA); Buckskin Horse (IBHA); and so on. (See page 134 for a list of some of these breed organizations.) When an unregistered horse has the color of a palomino, dun, pinto, paint, buckskin, and so on, the word is not capitalized.

Which Type?

Horses are usually described by *type* as well as by breed.

Horse type refers to the kind of work a horse is suited for. If you saw a horse that was well-muscled and kept his eyes calmly on the cows that were in front of him, no matter what his breed was, you would probably be looking at a stock type horse. If

An endurance horse is lean, and tough, and can cover many miles. *Example:* Arabian.

A hunter is a smooth, graceful horse that moves with a long, low reach of his legs. *Example:* American Thoroughbred.

A pleasure horse is a balanced, smooth-gaited horse that is easy to ride. *Example:* Individual horses in any breed.

A race horse is lean but tall, with a deep heart girth and exceptional speed. *Example:* American Thoroughbred.

A sport horse is a large and strong horse used for jumping, cross-country work, and dressage. *Example:* Trakehner.

A stock horse is well-muscled, quick on his feet, knows cows, has "cow sense." *Example:* American Quarter Horse.

A show horse has flashy, high-stepping gaits often used only in the show ring; also called animated. *Example:* Morgan or Saddlebred.

you saw a tall, lean horse flying like the wind through a pasture passing every other horse, you might be looking at a race type horse.

What Qualities and Characteristics?

Besides breed and type, there are other important qualities and characteristics to consider when choosing your horse.

Temperament and Manners

This should be first on your list of things to check. Look for a horse that is cooperative and calm. You need a horse that is alert but sensible. You wouldn't want your horse to jump sideways at every dog or piece of plastic that you pass. Be sure to avoid any horse with the bad habits of biting, kicking, rearing, bucking, or running away. Look for a horse that seems to enjoy people, not a horse that tries to avoid them.

Level of Training

In general, the more training a horse has, the more expensive he will be. If he has a show ring record, that will add even more to his price. You probably don't need a fancy show horse, but you do need a horse with good overall training so you can safely ride him at all gaits both in and out of an arena. You also need to be able to handle him safely from the ground. Such a horse will usually not be cheap because it takes a lot of time and effort to "make" a good horse.

Conformation and Movement

Conformation is the shape and form of your horse — how he is put together. Generally a horse with good

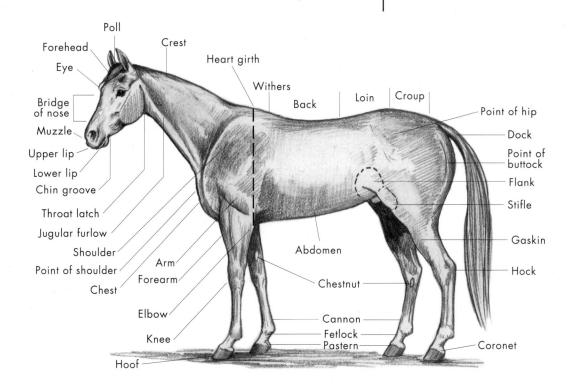

Parts of a horse

conformation moves well and has less of a chance of developing a lameness. If you want to show your horse, you'll probably want to look for good conformation **and** good looks!

It doesn't matter how pretty a horse is standing still. What is most important is that he moves well and is a comfortable riding horse. This depends on the horse's body type and build as well as his gaits. You'll need help from your riding instructor and veterinarian to help you learn how to evaluate a horse's movement.

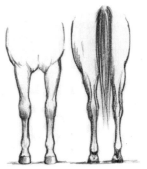

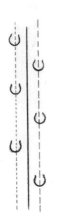

When horse's leg conformation is correct, travel is straight.

When horse's leg conformation is toed-out, travel is winging in.

When horse's leg conformation is toed-in, travel is paddling.

Observing leg conformation

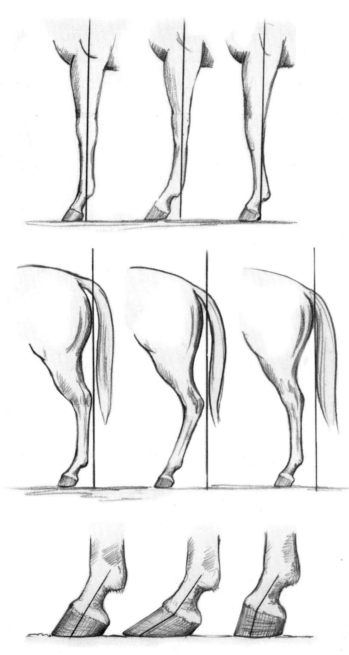

Correct leg and hoof conformation

Calf knee (top), sickle hock (middle), broken back hoof/ pastern axis (bottom)

Buck knee (top), post-legged (middle), broken forward hoof/ pastern axis (bottom)

Gaits

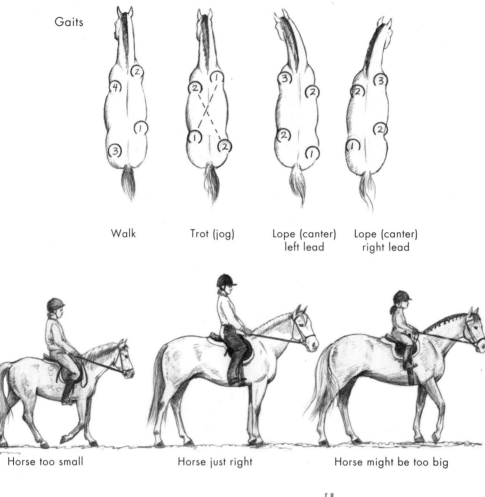

Walk   Trot (jog)   Lope (canter)
left lead   Lope (canter)
right lead

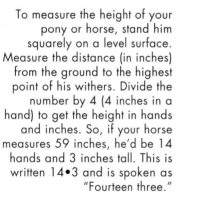

Horse too small   Horse just right   Horse might be too big

To measure the height of your pony or horse, stand him squarely on a level surface. Measure the distance (in inches) from the ground to the highest point of his withers. Divide the number by 4 (4 inches in a hand) to get the height in hands and inches. So, if your horse measures 59 inches, he'd be 14 hands and 3 inches tall. This is written 14•3 and is spoken as "Fourteen three."

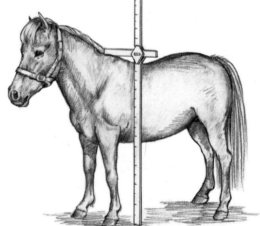

Size

When you are mounted on a horse or pony, your heels should not be below the horse's underline. If your legs are too long for a small pony, you have no way to give him correct leg signals — you'd be clicking your heels together under his belly! An adult pony or small horse will not grow any more, but *you* probably *will* get taller and grow longer legs. You don't want to outgrow your horse just when you've gotten used to each other. So, with your riding instructor's help, choose a horse that is big enough to last you for a while, a horse that you can "grow into."

Health

Never buy a sick horse hoping to nurse him back to health. It is just too time-consuming, expensive, and risky. If you find a horse that you really like but that is sick, tell the seller to call you when the horse recovers and you will consider looking at him again.

Your veterinarian can tell you if a horse has a clean bill of health when he gives the horse an examination before you buy him. This exam is called the pre-purchase exam. Read Chapter 5 very carefully so that you become familiar with common horse health problems such as founder, navicular disease, heaves, and strangles.

Soundness

A sound horse does not have a lameness or an illness that would prevent him from working. You will need an experienced horseperson and veterinarian to help you determine if a horse is sound. Don't buy an un-sound horse hoping he will get better. You need a horse that you can count on every day to perform without pain or sickness. Some perfectly sound horses have blemishes or scars that might look bad but don't

The Gaits

- Walk — the slowest gait, 4 *beats*

- Trot — a two-beat gait between a walk and a lope

- Jog — a very slow *Western* trot

- Canter — the *English* term for a three-beat gait; the Western term is lope

- Gallop — a very fast canter or lope; the horse is running

- Back — a two-beat gait in reverse

Beat. *A single step in a gait, involving one leg or two.*

Sex and Age Terms

How many of these words can you define? Write your definitions on a piece of paper, then check the Glossary on pages 141–148 to see how many you got right.

- broodmare
- colt
- dam
- filly
- foal
- gelding
- horse
- mare
- pony
- sire
- stallion
- stud
- suckling
- weanling
- yearling

affect how the horse moves or works. Sometimes you can get a good bargain on a horse with a blemish.

Sex

If you are buying your very first horse, I'd recommend a well-trained, quiet gelding because chances are he will behave the same from day to day. Because of heat cycles, some mares can be sweethearts one day and real grouches the next. So unless you are experienced or know that a particular mare is pretty even-tempered, I'd avoid a mare for a first horse. Under no circumstances should you consider handling a stallion until you are over 18 years of age, have the permission of your parents, and have professional guidance. Stallions can be dangerous for you to handle because they are usually full of energy and excitable, especially around other horses.

Age

For safety, your first horse should be at least 8 years old, but could be as old as 20 or more. If a horse has been well trained and well cared for, the older he is, the more steady and trustworthy he is. Some horses continue performing well into their twenties. Horses under five years of age are often unpredictable and their training is not solid enough to be trustworthy for a beginning rider.

Color

Color and markings should be the last things you consider when choosing your horse. The best color is "kind and well trained." Still, horses come in many different colors and color combinations, and there are special terms to describe many of them.

Bay

The body color of a bay ranges from tan to reddish-brown, with black mane and tail, and usually black on the lower legs.

Black

Black means true black over the entire body, except there may be white leg and face markings. The mane and tail are black.

Blue roan

A blue roan horse has a uniform mixture of black and white hairs all over the body. The horse is born this way and stays this color all its life. (The color does not get lighter as the horse gets older the way the coat of a gray horse does.) The head and legs are usually darker than the body. There can be a few red hairs in the mixture.

Brown

A brown horse has mixed black and brown hair. The mane, tail, and legs are black. A brown horse often appears black but has light areas around the eyes, *muzzle, flank,* and inside the upper portions of the legs.

Buckskin

A buckskin is tan, yellow, or gold with a black mane and tail and black lower legs. Buckskins do not have dorsal stripes as duns do (see next page).

Chestnut

The body, mane, and tail of a chestnut are various shades of golden brown, from sunny gold to reddish brown. The mane and tail of some chestnuts are the same color as the body. When the mane and tail are lighter than the body they are called *flaxen.*

Muzzle. *The end of a horse's face, including the nose, nostrils, and lips.*

Flank. *The area of a horse's barrel between the rib cage and the hindquarters.*

Flaxen. *A golden mane or tail on a darker-bodied horse.*

Star   Snip   Strip   Star and strip

Star and   Bald   Chin spot
narrow blaze

Face markings

Dun

Dun means yellow or gold body and leg color, often
with black or brown mane and tail. A dun usually has a
dorsal stripe (stripe down the back), zebra stripes on
the legs, and stripes over the withers.

Gray

A gray has black skin with a mixture of black and white
hairs. The horse is usually dark when it is born (black
or charcoal gray) and gets lighter each year until it is
almost white.

Grullo

Grullo is a type of dun with a smoky or mouse-colored body (each hair is this color; it is not a mixture of dark and light hairs). The mane and tail and the lower legs are usually black. There is usually a black dorsal stripe.

Liver chestnut

This is a very dark red chestnut color. The mane, tail, and legs are the same color as the body or flaxen.

Palomino

Palomino means a golden coat with a white or light mane and tail.

Red dun

A red dun has a yellowish, light red, or pinkish-tan body. The mane and tail are reddish, flaxen, white, or mixed. There is usually a red dorsal stripe and usually red stripes on the legs and withers.

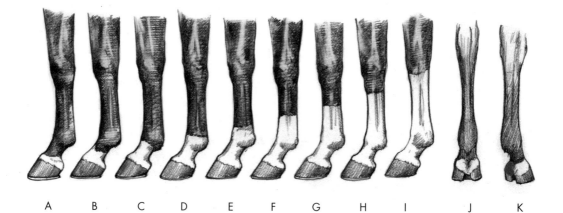

Leg Markings: A, coronet; B, half-pastern; C, pastern; D, high pastern; E, ankle or sock; F, sock; G, half-stocking; H, ¾ stocking; I, stocking; J, heel; K, half-heel.

Sorrel

Sorrel is a Western term used to describe a reddish or copper-red body with mane and tail the same color as the body or flaxen.

Strawberry roan or red roan

This is a mixture of red and white hairs all over the horse's body but usually darker on the head and legs. The mane and tail can be red, black, or flaxen.

Horsekeeping

A horse's shelter requirements are pretty basic. In the summer, be sure there is a place for your horse to get shade, either from a shed, barn, or some trees. When flies are bad, help him ward them off with a fly sheet, a mask, and the careful use of fly spray. (See Chapters 5 and 6 for more information.)

In the winter, when temperatures drop below 50°F, make sure your horse doesn't get chilled. If it is raining or snowing and there is a wind, your horse should have shelter, or as an alternative, he should wear a storm blanket. (See Chapter 6.)

Your horse can't go get a glass of water when he is thirsty or put on a jacket when he gets cold. He depends on you. Be sure he has what he needs for good health and comfort. Whether you are keeping your horse at home or at a boarding stable, his welfare is your responsibility.

How you take care of your horse depends on where he lives — on pasture or in a pen or paddock.

Keeping a Horse on Pasture

This is the most natural way to keep your horse, but it has disadvantages as well as advantages.

Advantages

Pasture living allows your horse to have free exercise, fresh air, and sunshine. If there are other horses there, pasture living allows your horse to socialize. Depending

1. Standing, dozing on three legs. This is how horses spend most of their resting time.

2. Lying down on his belly with his legs tucked under. A horse can stand up from this position in a matter of seconds.

3. Lying on his side with his legs stretched out.

Note: If your horse spends more than a few hours each day lying down, he may be causing too much pressure on his legs and intestines which could lead to problems. You will need to find out why he is lying down so much. He may be lame or ill.

on the quality of the pasture, a horse might get all or just a part of his feed needs met by eating pasture grass. Many horses stay more mentally content on pasture than if they are kept in pens or stalls. You will probably have fewer daily chores if your horse is on pasture because you won't have a stall to clean.

Disadvantages

The reason not all horses can be kept on pasture is that land is very expensive and horses are very hard on land. In some areas, such as Iowa and other Midwestern states, pastures are so lush that one acre provides plenty of grass for one horse. In other areas, such as the dry ranges of Wyoming or the desert of New Mexico, pastures are very dry and thin and it might take more than 50 acres to provide enough grass for one horse. You will need to talk with your county Extension agent to find out how many horses your pasture can support. (See Chapter 8 to learn how to find your county agent.)

If you keep your horse on pasture with other horses, he might become so closely bonded to the other horses in the herd that he's hard to catch and resists being taken away from the others when you want to go for a ride.

Some horses are very grouchy. When put in a pasture with other horses, they might kick and fight. If your horse is grouchy or has to share a pasture with a grouchy horse, he could be injured.

If there is more than one horse on the pasture, it is difficult to be sure that each one is getting the appropriate amount of hay or grain for feed.

It usually takes more time to catch and groom a horse kept on pasture, which means it takes longer to get ready for riding.

Flies are more of a problem for horses on pasture because damp, grassy areas provide good breeding grounds for flies.

The most serious disadvantage to keeping a horse on pasture is probably that, like most horses, he may not know when to quit eating and can get very fat. When a horse eats too much, he can get a very bad stomachache, called colic, or he could founder, which is a very serious lameness affecting the hooves. Both conditions are described in Chapter 5.

Pasture Size

Contact your county Extension agent to find out how many horses your pasture can support and never put more horses on it than that. If you have two or more pastures, rotate your horses between the pastures so the grasses have a time to regrow.

Fences and Gates

Make sure your fences are safe so your horse does not get hurt. There are many types of safe horse fence, such as wooden board, post and rail, pipe. Whatever type you choose, be sure it is at least 5 feet high; 6 feet high is much better. You should check the fence routinely for damage.

There are many kinds of safe horse fencing and here is one example. (However, this horse should not have been turned out wearing a halter because of the risk of him getting his halter caught on a fence, tree, or his own hoof or shoe when scratching or rolling.)

Horses like to hang around gates, waiting to be fed or wanting to be groomed and ridden. These "gate potatoes" often crowd the gate area or press over the top of the gate. And when play gets rough, they might push right through the gate. That's why the gate must be at least as tall as the fence, must be made of very safe, strong material, and must be securely latched with a horse-proof latch. Horses are pretty quick learners when it comes to opening gates.

Barbed wire should never be used for fencing with horses. This gate is not strong enough and does not latch securely enough for use with horses.

Fence Safety Tips

- Replace barbed wire with safe horse fencing.

- Repair broken boards.

- Remove and replace nails that are sticking out.

- Replace fence that is lower than 4 feet tall (unless you only have small ponies).

- Immediately treat any wood that shows chewing.

If your horse gets loose, whether he jumps the fence or walks out a gate that was left open, you are responsible for any trouble he might get into. If he ruins your neighbor's prize garden or walks out on the road and is hit by a car, you are responsible. That is why it is important to keep all gates securely latched and to maintain fence safety.

Keeping Your Horse in a Stall

Horses that must live indoors are healthiest and happiest when the building has lots of fresh air but is draft free and dry. An airtight, heated barn is usually damp and very unhealthy for horses.

Stall Size

A box stall that is 12-feet-by-10-feet works well for many horses; larger horses (over 16 hands) will require a 12 x 12 or 12 x 14 stall. Arabians often are comfortable in a 10-foot-by-10-foot stall. Ponies can get along in stalls 8-feet-by-10-feet or smaller, depending on the size of the pony.

Stall Floor

The stall floor should be a well-draining material such as a mixture of very small gravel and a sandy dirt. If you can, add mats or perforated stall flooring over the soil. This helps keep your horse cleaner and drier. You still need to use bedding with flooring, but you will use much less. And with stall flooring, the stall won't develop huge craters.

Bedding

The type of bedding you use depends on what is available in your area. Wood shavings, straw, and peanut or rice hulls all make good horse bedding. Try the types that are available in your area and compare how much they cost, how long they last, and how comfortable they are for your horse.

Exercise

When a horse lives in a stall, you must be sure he gets exercise every day. The best kind of exercise for a stalled horse is at least one hour per day of continuous, controlled exercise such as riding, *longeing,* or driving. If you just turn your horse out for exercise, he may take one gallop to his favorite corner of the pasture and eat. If a horse has not been exercised for a few days and you turn him loose, he may run and play so hard to burn off his extra energy that he injures himself.

Grooming and Blanketing

Horses in stalls are right there when you want to ride and are usually clean enough to only need a normal grooming. If you blanket a stalled horse, he will tend

There are many types of stalls and stall doors for horses. Choose one that is safe and comfortable for your horse. This type of stall door allows a horse to look out of his stall at other horses and not feel so confined or lonely. However, if you need to lead a horse down an aisle of a barn with stall doors like these, the stalled horses can reach out and bother you or the horse you are leading.

Longe. To work a horse around you in a circle on a 30-foot line at various gaits.

Danger!

Metal farm panels are often used to make temporary, moveable pens. Some of these panels are very dangerous. They can trap a horse's legs when he rolls near them. If the panels are shorter than 5 feet tall, a horse can get his legs over the top if he bucks and rears in his pen. Also, a horse can get a leg caught between certain types of panels. Choose your panels carefully.

to grow less winter hair. This makes grooming easier and also lets the horse cool out more quickly after exercise. But once you blanket a horse in the fall, you should keep him blanketed all winter. It wouldn't be fair to turn him out in the cold weather without a blanket once he has gotten used to it. See Chapter 6 for more information on blankets.

Keeping Your Horse in a Pen or Paddock

A *pen* or *paddock* is a good compromise between keeping your horse in a stall and keeping him in a pasture.

Pen

A pen is an outdoor living space for your horse that is at least 24-feet-by-24-feet. (This is the size of about four stalls put together.) A pen does not have grass growing in it.

An open-front shed with exercise pen is a popular, low-maintenance way of keeping a horse.

Paddock

A paddock is a small pasture that can be anywhere from about ¼ acre to 1 acre in size. Besides providing exercise, a paddock might also provide some grazing.

Run

A *run* is a long, narrow fenced-in area that is usually attached to a stall. A common-sized run is about 12-feet-by-60-feet or longer. This allows a horse to trot a few strides, turn around, and come back.

Run. A long, narrow fenced-in area usually attached to a stall.

Exercise

If the pen, run, or paddock is large enough that your horse exercises by himself, then you might not have to take him out of the pen for extra exercise every day. But even if your horse's pen is fairly large, you still should take him out for riding or longeing at least three or four times per week.

A paddock is an enclosed grassy area of an acre or less that has safe fencing.

Feeding

CHAPTER 4

Basic Nutrients

The five types of nutrients you must provide for your horse are: water, carbohydrates, protein, minerals, and vitamins.

Water

Horses drink from 5 to 20 gallons or more of water per day. Clean, fresh water should be available to your horse 24 hours a day, every day. Your horse should not be expected to quench his thirst by eating snow. It would take him a very long time to get enough water that way, and it would make him very cold inside.

Your horse will drink more water than normal if:

- The weather is very hot or humid

- He is exercised hard

- He is eating a lot of salt

- He is eating alfalfa hay

Carbohydrates

Horses get energy from the carbohydrates (starches and sugars) in their hay and grain. How much energy feed your horse needs depends on his age, weight, and his level of activity.

Protein

Protein is necessary for all horses but especially for young growing horses. A horse may not grow properly if he isn't fed enough of the right kind of protein. If he is fed too much protein, his bones may grow abnormally. Also, the excess protein will have to be expelled in his urine. A horse that is fed too much protein drinks more water than normal and urinates more than normal. Feeding too much protein is not only wasteful, it may be dangerous for a young horse and it might be hard on any horse's kidneys, too.

Minerals

Minerals are important for many of your horse's body functions. All horses should have free-choice trace mineral salt. Free choice means that your horse should be able to get to the mineral salt at all times and eat all he wants. Many horses need extra calcium and phosphorus in their diets as well, so you should consider purchasing a trace mineral salt block that has 12% calcium and 12% phosphorous added to it.

Vitamins

Vitamins are present in the hay and grain a horse normally eats. You rarely need to add vitamins to your horse's feed.

Types of Feeds

Feed for horses comes in three forms: hay, grain, and block.

Hay

A horse's digestive system is designed to mainly digest bulky food like hay and pasture.

Grass Hay

Grass is the traditional horse hay and includes timothy, brome, orchard grass, and others. When grass hay is baled properly it makes good horse feed. If it is too mature when it is baled, it is not much better than straw.

Alfalfa Hay

Alfalfa hay is higher in protein than grass hay. It has three times the amount of calcium and many more vitamins than grass. Alfalfa is often used to feed growing young horses, because, as you know, calcium is good for bones. However, alfalfa has so much calcium that it can cause problems with bone growth. For that reason, you should check with your Extension agent or veterinarian before you begin feeding alfalfa.

Pasture

Pasture provides necessary exercise and nutrients for horses. To make best use of a pasture, let your horse eat it when it is 4 to 6 inches tall. After he has grazed it down, move him to another pasture.

Native pasture is what appears on the land without extra seeds being planted by people. When you drive through parts of Wyoming, all you see is native pasture. Improved pasture is a field that has had special pasture grass seeds planted. Usually improved pastures are watered or irrigated. If you have improved pasture, one acre could support two horses during the six-month grazing season of spring, summer, and fall. However, it may require 50 or more acres of native dry range land to support a single horse.

Grain

Many horses do not need to be fed grain. Young horses, horses in hard work, pregnant mares, and mares with foals usually need grain and supplements.

Straw

Straw is what is left over after oats are harvested. It is used for bedding, not feed. It is basically a bunch of very dry hollow stems with very little nutrition. Good straw is a bright, shiny golden yellow.

Good Hay

Good hay is free of mold, dust, and weeds. It has a bright green color and a fresh smell. It is leafy, soft, and dry but not brittle. There is no dampness that could lead to spoilage or molding.

1. Know how much
   your horse weighs.

2. Know how many
   pounds of hay he
   should be fed.

3. Know how many
   pounds of grain
   he needs.

4. Don't overfeed
   your horse.

5. Don't underfeed
   your horse.

6. Know what mineral
   supplements your
   horse needs.

7. Feed your horse at
   least twice a day.

8. Feed him at the
   same time every day.

9. Be sure he always
   has fresh water.

10. Make any changes to
    his feed very gradually.

11. Introduce your
    horse to pasture
    grass very gradually.

12. Never feed or water
    a horse that is hot
    from exercise.

Oats

Oats are the traditional, safe horse grain because they provide the right balance of fiber (from their hulls) and energy (from the kernel).

Corn

Corn has a very thin covering that does not provide much fiber, but the kernel does provide a great deal of energy. Corn can be too concentrated for some horses. A can of corn has twice the energy content as the same can of oats. That is why you should never just feed by the "can" method. (See page 48 for more details on how much to feed your horse.)

Commercial Grain Mixtures

Commercially prepared horse feeds are available as pellets or grain mixes. Pellets might have both hay and grain in them. "Sweet feed" grain mixes are usually made up of oats or barley and corn, molasses, and a protein pellet. Feed companies create different products for different horse groups. You can find special feed for foals, yearlings, performance horses, broodmares, and even for senior horses. When you feed commercial grain mixtures, be sure to carefully weigh each horse's amount on a scale; do not carelessly feed your horse a scoop of feed and not know how much it weighs.

Mineral and Protein Block

Mineral and protein blocks provide nutrients that supplement your horse's main diet of hay or grain.

Trace Mineral Salt

A trace mineral salt block contains the same kind of salt you use on your food, with other important minerals added. It is usually a red block. Your horse should be able to get to a trace mineral salt block at all times and should be allowed to eat as much as he wants.

Molasses Protein Block

A molasses protein block is usually brown and is like a big candy bar for horses. It also contains salt. Your horse will probably gulp down one of these blocks in a few days if you don't roll it out of his reach. You should only use a protein block if the hay you are feeding is very low in protein. Then you must watch to make sure that your horse doesn't eat too much of the block at one time. If he gobbles a half a block in one day, he might *colic,* have diarrhea, or become dehydrated from eating too much molasses or salt.

Colic. *Intestinal discomfort.*

Calcium and Phosphorus Block

Calcium and phosphorus are very important minerals for all horses. The extra amount a horse should get depends on what kind of hay you are feeding and how old the horse is. Most of the time a horse's calcium and phosphorus needs can be met with a 12 percent calcium and 12 percent phosphorus block (sometimes called a 12:12 block). Ask your feed store for help deciding what type of block your horse needs.

Following the Twelve Rules of Horse Feeding

Here's what you need to know to feed your horse properly.

1. Know How Much Your Horse Weighs

You can't feed your horse properly unless you know how much he weighs. Since your horse is too big for your bathroom scale, you need another way to determine his weight. If you measure his heart girth (see page 47) with a special horse weight tape, it will tell

Salt and mineral blocks should be available to your horse "free-choice" so he can have them whenever he wants.

you how much he weighs. If you don't have a horse weight tape, you can use an ordinary measuring tape and find out approximately how much your pony or horse weighs by referring to the following table.

Heart girth (in inches)	Weight (in pounds)
54	492
56	531
58	596
60	664
62	722
64	785
66	852
68	902
70	985
72	1065
74	1220
76	1265

2. Know How Many Pounds of Hay Your Horse Needs

Your horse feels the best when his ration consists of a high percentage of bulk (hay) and a low percentage of concentrate (grain). Be careful not to feed too much grain.

For every 100 pounds your horse weighs, feed him about 1.5 pounds of hay per day. If your horse weighs 1000 pounds, that is 10 times 100 pounds. He should get 15 pounds of hay per day (1.5 pounds of hay x 10). Since you will probably feed your horse twice a day,

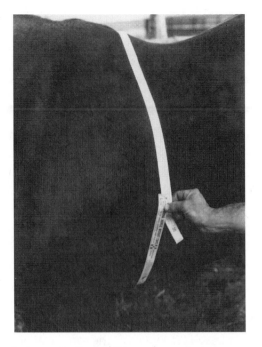

The easiest way to "weigh" your horse is to use a special
weight tape. Place the tape around the horse's heart girth
just behind the withers. Be sure the tape is lying flat.
Read the number of pounds indicated on the tape.

split his hay ration in half. A 1000-pound horse would
get 7.5 pounds of hay in the morning and 7.5 pounds
in the evening.

You should weigh the hay at each feeding because
flakes of hay can vary. For example, one flake might
weigh 2 pounds and the next one 7 pounds. That's why
if you simply feed your horse two flakes of hay, you
really don't know how much you are feeding him.

3. Know How Many Pounds of Grain Your Horse Needs

Not all horses require grain in their diet. Grain should
be fed to young, growing horses, horses in moderate to
hard work (one or more hours of active riding per day),
and lactating broodmares (mares that have nursing

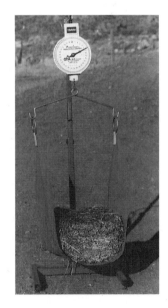

Because flakes of hay
can vary in weight, it is
best to weigh each
feeding of hay to be sure
your horse is getting
enough but not too much
hay to eat.

If you have three horses on pasture, place the feed in four or more piles that are far enough apart from each other so that the horses won't fight over them.

How Much Does It Weigh?

Each grain has its own weight. When you fill a quart-sized can with one of the following grains commonly fed to horses, here is how much it will weigh:

Bran = .5 pound
Oats = 1 pound
Barley = 1.5 pounds
Corn = 1.75 pounds

foals). Feed each horse his grain individually according to his specific needs. This avoids competition, fighting, and some horses gulping and getting too much while others get very little.

Grain should be fed by weight, not volume. Don't use a scoop to measure the amount of grain unless you know exactly how much a scoop of grain weighs. Instead of feeding by the can or scoop method, feed your horse by weighing his grain. First weigh the can. Write down how much the can weighs — for example, 1.2 pounds. Then fill the can with grain and weigh it. If the empty can weighs 1.2 pounds and the can with grain weighs 4.2 pounds, that means there are 3 pounds of grain inside the can.

Compare how much the same size can would hold of bran, sweet feed, oats, pellets, and other horse feeds. Oats are much lighter than corn, for example, so a can of oats will weigh far less than the same can of corn.

Each feeding of grain should be weighed carefully.

4. Don't Overfeed Your Horse

Although it is tempting to show your horse how much you love him by giving him extra feed, this is often the worst thing you can do. He might *founder* or colic. When a horse feels sick, he cannot throw up. He will have to wait until the feed that is making him sick passes through his digestive system.

To prevent your horse from accidentally overeating, be sure your grain room has a secure lock on it. If your horse was able to get into the grain room, he would probably eat himself sick and suffer colic or founder. (See Chapter 5.)

Overfeeding can also make your horse gain too much weight. If your horse is overweight, he has more stress on his legs, which could contribute to his becoming lame.

5. Don't Underfeed Your Horse

If you don't feed your horse enough, he could get too thin and weak, be cold all of the time, lack energy, and be unable to ward off sickness.

6. Know What Mineral Supplements Your Horse Needs

Balance your horse's feed ration by providing free-choice trace mineralized salt. Trace mineralized salt contains sodium chloride (salt), and usually iodine, zinc, iron, manganese, copper, and cobalt.

Depending on the horse's age and the type of hay he is getting, he might need additional calcium and phosphorus. The best way to be sure your horse is getting what he needs is to provide him with free-choice access to a calcium and phosphorus mineral block that is made specifically for horses.

However, if you are feeding only grass hay and grain to a very young horse (under the age of 2), you might

Founder. Another word for laminitis, a serious disease affecting a horse's hooves and caused by a horse's eating too much grain or green pasture.

Feed Records

You should always have a record of what each of your horses gets to eat. This way, if you have to be away from home and someone else has to feed your horses for you, that person will know what to do. A blackboard in your feed room works really well for this.

need to provide him with an extra source of calcium because both grass hay and grain have more phosphorus in them than calcium. On the other hand, if you are feeding a young horse only alfalfa hay, which is very rich in calcium, you might need to add some phosphorus to his diet to balance the minerals. Ask your veterinarian or county Extension agent to help you evaluate the hay and grain you are feeding so you will know what type of mineral you should add to your horse's ration. If you don't know what type of hay you are feeding, contact your county agent and he can either evaluate it for you or tell you where you can get your hay tested.

7. Feed Your Horse at Least Twice a Day

Since horses evolved as wandering grazers, their systems are geared to many small meals each day. That is why you should feed your horse two to three times each day.

If your horse gulps his grain as soon as you give it to him, feed him his hay first to take the edge off his appetite. If he is still hurrying, add some rocks about the size of golf balls to his grain to slow him down. Feeding him his grain in a large shallow pan will make him eat more slowly than if you feed his grain in a small, deep bucket that allows him to gobble.

8. Feed Your Horse at the Same Time Every Day

Horses have an extremely strong biological clock, especially when it comes to feeding. Feeding late or inconsistently can result in colic and other digestive upsets. Be sure to feed the same amounts at the same time every day.

Near your feeding area, you should have a feed board
that lists what each horse should get to eat: how many
pounds of hay and how many pounds of grain.
That way, if someone needs to feed your horses for you,
there will be instructions.

9. Be Sure Your Horse Always Has Fresh Water

Always make sure your horse has good quality, free-
choice water. Your horse might not necessarily drink
when it is convenient for you. Instead, he will drink as
part of his daily routine, usually an hour or two after
eating hay. If your horse does not get enough water, he
can lose his appetite and suffer a bout of colic.

In winter, a horse should not be expected to eat
snow or ice for water. The best routine in winter is to
draw fresh water for your horse every day. If you live in
a cold climate and if your horse is out on a pasture
with a creek, you may need to break the ice to keep the
water hole open so your horse can drink.

Prevent "Tying Up"

If you feed your horse 2 pounds of grain or more per feeding and you have not exercised him for a few days, be very careful when you start him up. Be sure to warm him up very slowly. If you suddenly got on him and galloped off, his muscles might cramp and cause him severe pain and damage. This is called "tying-up" (see Chapter 5). To prevent tying up, decrease your horse's grain ration during periods of inactivity. Then when he is back to regular work, return his ration gradually to its regular level.

10. Make Changes to Your Horse's Feed Very Gradually

Make all changes in feed gradually. Whether you are changing the **type** of feed or the **amount** being fed, make only small changes. Maintain the new level for several feedings before making another small change. For example, if you are feeding 2 pounds of grain per feeding and want the ration to be increased to 3 pounds per feeding, increase to 2½ pounds per feeding and feed that for at least two days. Then increase to 3 pounds.

If you are making a change in hays, start by replacing ¼ of the "old" hay in the hay ration with new hay. Feed this combination for two days. Then increase the amount of new hay so that the hay ration is ½ old hay and ½ new hay for two days. Then feed ¼ ration of old hay and ¾ ration new hay for 2 days. Finally, feed all new hay.

11. Introduce Pasture Grass Very Gradually

When turning a horse out to pasture for the first time, be sure he has had a full feed of hay. Limit his grazing time to one-half hour per day for the first two days. Then he can be on pasture one-half hour twice a day for two days, then one hour twice a day, and so on. Keep a close watch on a horse that is on pasture. A horse that eats too much rich or green feed can quickly become overweight or suffer laminitis (founder), a devastating condition.

12. Never Feed or Water a Horse When He Is Hot from Exercise

Do not feed a horse immediately after hard work and do not work a horse until at least one hour after a full feed. The horse has a sensitive digestive system, and

you must be considerate in his work requirements around meal times. When a horse is
hot from exercise, let him take only very
small sips of water. If you have just come back
from a trail ride and your horse is breathing
very hard, walk him for a few minutes and let
him take a few sips of cool water. (Very cold
water could be too much of a shock to his
system.) Then walk him for a few more
minutes. Then offer him a few more sips of
water and so on. When you feel his breathing
is normal and he has cooled down, you can
feed him some grass hay.

A hay and grain feeder
for a stall or pen

Feeders

Don't feed a horse on sandy or loose soil. If a horse eats
sand or dirt with his feed, he can suffer *sand colic*.
Sand colic results from a large amount of sand or dirt
accumulating at the bottom of the horse's intestine.
The dirt slows down and clogs up the
horse's digestive system (see page 70).

Feeder Care

Be sure your horse's feeders are
clean and safe. Do not let feed
accumulate in the bottom of feeders.
Moldy or spoiled feed can create
problems for your horse and lead to
large veterinary bills for you. Routinely check all feeders for sharp
edges, broken parts, loose wires, or
nails or any other hazard. If you use
hay nets, tie them securely and high
enough so your horse cannot get his
leg caught in the net.

A grain feeder that
can be used with a
wooden fence

When tying up a hay net, run the tie string through the tie ring, then through the bottom of the hay net, then back up through the tie ring. The hay net should be tied high enough so that when it is empty, the net does not hang so low that the horse could get his legs tangled in it.

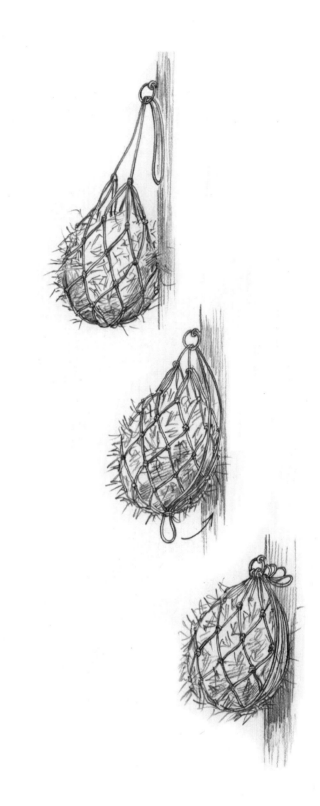

Feed Storage

Proper storage of your horse's hay and grain is an important part of horsekeeping.

Storing Grain

Grain should be stored in a mouse-proof, locked grain room. If your grain room is not tight enough to be mouse-free, then store your grain in metal or heavy plastic barrels and let your cat roam around the feed room to keep the mice away.

Storing Hay

Before storing hay, be sure it is fully cured and dry. Ideally, hay should be stored indoors, stacked on wooden pallets to keep it from lying on the moist ground. If you must store hay outdoors, stack it very tightly on pallets, and cover it with a tarp.

Store grain in mouse-proof cans or barrels. If the barrels are not in a locked room, outfit the lids with straps to prevent your horse from knocking the lids off and over-eating.

Fifteen tons of hay protected from the weather.

Health Care

Daily Health Check

In order to perform a daily health check, you need to learn the signs of a healthy horse and signs of an unhealthy horse. Once you know what to look for, you should be able to make a daily check in a couple of minutes. First you need to know what is normal for horses in general. Then you need to know what is normal for **your** horse. Just like kids, every horse is different.

How Is He Standing?

First, look at how your horse is standing. Is his head down or up? If it is down, he might just be dozing or he might be feeling sick. Is he holding one leg up? If it is a hind leg, he might be resting it while he is sleeping, or it might be lame. If he is holding up a front leg, it probably is lame.

How Is He Lying Down?

If your horse is lying down, **how** is he lying down? Is he in a normal, peaceful sleeping position? Or is he restless and rolling back and forth?

Caution

If your horse likes to lie down on his side and roll, he might get his legs trapped in a pen or stall.

What Is His Expression?

What is the expression on your horse's face? Is he alert, with ears forward and bright eyes? Does he look content? Or does he look dull or nervous?

Check His Legs

Next, look carefully at your horse's legs. Look for wounds and also for swelling or puffiness. If you notice something out of the ordinary, you should halter your horse and examine his legs by feeling them. You'll need to develop a feel for what is normal for the texture and temperature of a horse's legs in general and what is normal for **your** horse's legs. When your horse moves, does he place his weight on all four legs equally or does he limp? Does he bob his head, skip, or buckle over at the hoof? Does he take short, stiff steps? All of these can indicate a lameness problem.

Check His Appetite and Thirst

Has your horse finished all of his feed from the previous feeding? Has he been drinking plenty of water? Is he standing by his feeder at feeding time waiting for his next meal? A good appetite is one of the signs of good health. Your horse should finish all of his food 2 to 3 hours after you feed him.

Check His Manure

What does your horse's manure look like? The fecal balls should be well formed, but they should easily break in half. If the fecal balls are very dry and hard, the horse is not drinking enough water. Loose sloppy piles (more like "cow pies") tell you that your horse's feed is either too rich (too much grain or alfalfa hay), he is eating too much salt and water, or he has an irritation in his digestive tract and has diarrhea.

If you see slime or mucus on his manure, he has an irritated gut. If there is whole grain in the manure or long pieces of fiber from hay, it means the horse is either gobbling his feed without chewing, that the feed is passing through his body too fast, or that he has a dental problem and can't chew his feed thoroughly.

If you see worms in his manure, this tells you that it is way past time for you to deworm him.

Other Health Clues

Look at your horse's stall or pen and his body for signs of rubbing, rolling, or pawing. Is his tail ruffled? Is he covered with dirt or manure? Is he sweaty? Are there holes in his stall from pawing? If you have reason to suspect there might be a problem such as colic, you should check your horse's vital signs. These are things you can learn how to do from your veterinarian.

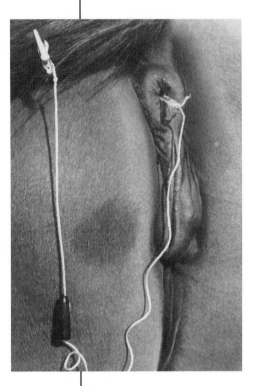

Your Horse's Vital Signs

Learning how to check and evaluate your horse's vital signs will give you important information about your horse's health.

Temperature

The average temperature of an adult horse at rest is about 100°F. The normal range is usually 99°F to 101°F. Ask your 4-H leader or veterinarian to teach you how to lubricate a thermometer with petroleum jelly or a drop of saliva and insert it into the horse's rectum. Leave the thermometer there for two to three minutes before taking a reading.

When taking your horse's temperature, use a farm animal thermometer with a string tied to it and a clip on the other end of the string. Clip the string to the horse's tail so that if the thermometer falls out, it won't land on the ground and break.

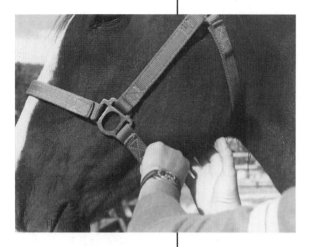

One of the places you can take a horse's pulse is under the jaw. As you count the pulse beats, use a watch with a second hand so you can tell when 60 seconds have passed.

Fetlock. *The joint between the pastern and the cannon. (See the illustration on page 23.)*

Pulse

The average pulse rate of an adult horse at rest is about 35 to 40 beats per minute. Young horses have much higher pulse rates. A two-week-old foal's pulse can be as high as 100 beats and a two-year-old's 40 to 50 beats per minute. If your horse is excited, in pain, nervous, has a high temperature, is in shock, has a disease, or has just completed exercise, his pulse rate will be higher than normal.

Pulse rates can be taken at the horse's jaw or just above the *fetlock.*

Respiration

The average respiration rate of an adult horse at rest is 12 to 25 breaths per minute. One inhalation (breathing in) and one exhalation (breathing out) are counted as one breath.

To measure your horse's breathing rate, watch his flank area and count every time he breathes in as one breath. This will be easier to see after your horse has exercised than when he is resting. It takes a lot of practice to be able to get an accurate respiration count when a horse is resting.

Daily Routine

By following the same routine of feeding, grooming, and exercise every day, you will help keep your horse healthy and you will be aware of any changes that indicate a possible health problem.

In the morning, feed your horse his hay and give him a quick check. Feeding his hay first takes the edge off his appetite and decreases the chance that he will gulp his grain. Be sure he has enough water and that it is clean. Feed the grain ration. Sometime after your horse has finished his morning ration, take him out of the stall or pen and tie him in a grooming area. As you pick out his hooves and groom him, give him a closer check. Then either turn him out for his daily exercise or ride him. Clean the stall or pen (described later in this chapter). Either let it dry all day if your horse will be turned out or re-bed it so you can return your horse to his stall or pen. At the evening feeding, again, feed hay first, check the water, and then feed grain.

If your daily chores involve pasture horses, you will have a different routine. Just because pasture horses might be farther away and you don't see them as often, don't forget them. Be sure you see them every day and give each one a thorough check.

Teach your pasture horses to respond to a call or whistle by feeding them when they come.

Keeping Your Horse's Health Record Book

You'll need to keep a record of your horse's health care. You can use a little notebook or a card file (like a recipe box) to write down the important information. For each horse, you should keep complete records on health care, farrier work, training, and breeding. Jotting everything on one calendar instead of in a notebook usually doesn't work very well. However, using a calendar is a handy way to remind yourself when you have to deworm your horse or when your farrier is coming.

Besides keeping daily records, you need to keep a file folder of important documents in a safe place in your house. In this folder keep such things as the horse's registration papers, the bill of sale you got when you bought the horse to show that you own him, a brand inspection certificate, a registration of his tattoo or freeze branding, his pedigree, his insurance policy, and any important test results such as the *Coggins test* for Equine Infectious Anemia. Also in the folder you should keep at least four very clear photos of your horse showing him from each side and from the front and rear. That way, if your horse ever wanders down the road or is stolen, you will have a way to identify him to the police.

SEPTEMBER

SUNDAY	MONDAY	TUESDAY	WEDNESDAY	THURSDAY	FRIDAY	SATURDAY
				1	2	3 *10 am Farrier Appointment*
4	5	6	7	8	9	10
11	12 *Deworm Diamond (get mom to help)*	13	14	15	16	17
18	19	20	21	22	23	24 *9 am Vet Appointment Float teeth Fall vaccinations*
25	26	27	28	29	30	

Protecting Your Horse from Parasites

Parasite. A harmful organism that lives on or in another organism.

Parasites are a common health problem for horses. You should learn about the kinds of parasites that might threaten your horse's health and how to protect your horse from them.

Internal Parasites

All horses have internal parasites, which means they live inside the horse's body.

Worms

One type of internal parasite is a worm that hatches from worm eggs in your horse's manure. All horse manure contains worm eggs. After the horse drops the manure on the ground, the worm eggs hatch. The tiny worm *larvae* are so small you can't easily see them. They crawl up on blades of grass and are eaten by the horse. Once they are inside the horse they become big worms which eat the horse's hay, grain, and even his blood while they live in his stomach and intestines. They lay eggs and continue the cycle. If worms are allowed to breed uncontrolled inside your horse, pretty soon there will be so many worms that the worms will get more of your horse's feed than he does.

The life cycle of most internal parasites starts with the horse eating larvae with his pasture or hay. Once inside the horse, the larvae develop into adult worms and lay eggs. The eggs are dropped on the ground with the horse's manure and hatch into larvae which the horse eats, starting the cycle all over again.

Bots

Besides worms, horses also have trouble with *bots*. Bots are similar to worms because they live inside the horse like worms do. But instead of hatching into larvae that crawl onto grass, bot *pupae* turn into bot flies. These flies look like bees (but they don't have stingers) and buzz around your horse. They lay eggs on the hair of his legs and body. The tiny yellow eggs appear in clusters that are easy to recognize. When your horse scratches his leg with his mouth, he swallows the eggs and the whole cycle starts all over again.

Bot block. *A rough,*
porous "stone" used to
scrub bot eggs off a
horse's hair.

When the bot flies are buzzing your horse, it can be very dangerous for you to handle your horse. One type of bot fly tries to fly up the horse's nose, which drives most horses crazy. The horse strikes at the flies with his front legs and runs frantically to get away from the bot flies. Be very careful in the late summer when the bot flies are around your horse. As soon as you see bot eggs in late summer or fall, remove them by scraping with a *bot block* (available at your farm supply store or tack shop) or a dull pocketknife.

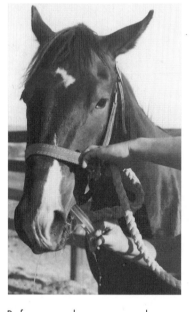 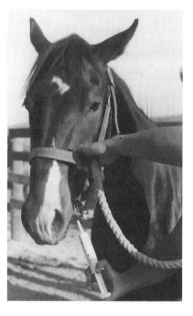

Before you deworm your horse, you might have to clean hay and grain out of his mouth. If you leave a wad of hay in his mouth, the dewormer will stick to the hay and he will spit out the medicine and the hay. To clean your horse's mouth, squirt some water into his mouth using a large plastic syringe with the needle removed. Let the water drip out completely before you give him the dewormer.

Ask your veterinarian to teach you how to deworm your horse. You will need to insert the dewormer syringe into the corner of his lips with the point of the syringe aiming upward just like you did with the syringe full of water.

Deworming

It is probably easy for you to see why you need to make a deworming plan and stick to it. Most horses need to be dewormed every two months to protect them from worms and bots. That's six times a year. Ask your veterinarian to help you make a plan and choose the dewormers you should use. If you watch your veterinarian very carefully, you can learn how to deworm your own horse.

External Parasites: Ticks and Lice

Pests that live on the outside of a horse's body are called external parasites. Lice and ticks live in a horse's coat. They like to burrow in the mane and tail and can make your horse itch like crazy. Ticks also carry Lyme disease, which is contagious to humans. If your horse rubs bald spots in his mane or tail, have your veterinarian check him for ticks or lice and recommend a treatment program.

Fungus and Other Skin Problems

Ringworm

Itching can also be caused by tiny organisms that grow on your horse's skin. Ringworm is a fungus that makes a horse's hair fall out in a patch the shape of a circle — that's how it got the name **ring**worm, even though it's not a worm at all.

Ringworm is contagious — you and your other horses can get it. If you have a horse with ringworm, take care of the problem immediately before it spreads. Clean the area with medicated soap and apply the ointment recommended by your veterinarian. Keep all grooming tools that you have used on the infected horse separate from other items. Wash them in the disinfectant recommended by your veterinarian.

Halters, blankets, stall walls, and fence posts (that your horse has rubbed on) will also carry the fungus, so you will need to disinfect them too.

Rain Rot

Another itchy skin problem is rain rot, which is usually caused by a bacteria. If your horse has crusty yellow scabs and bumps on his neck, back, and actually anywhere on his body, he probably has rain rot.

Treating Skin Problems

You will need your veterinarian's help in figuring out what is causing your horse to itch. Once she determines what it is, she will give you the proper medicated shampoo and instructions to cure your horse's problems. (See page 98 for information about giving your horse a bath.)

Vaccinating Your Horse Against Disease

At least once a year, your horse should receive vaccinations to protect him from getting certain diseases. Ask your veterinarian what vaccinations your horse should get. It will depend on where you live. Almost all horses should be vaccinated against tetanus, encephalomyelitis, influenza, and rhinopneumonitis. In some parts of the country your horse will also need to be vaccinated against Potomac horse fever, rabies, and strangles.

Tetanus

The common name for this disease is "lockjaw." It is an infection of the nervous system. The bacteria that cause tetanus enter the horse's body through a wound (usually a hoof wound) or through the umbilical cord that is attached to a foal's belly button. The muscles of a horse with lockjaw stiffen up so severely that within a few days he dies or must be put to sleep. A yearly tetanus vaccination will protect your horse from this horrible disease.

Encephalomyelitis

The common name for this disease is "sleeping sickness." It is caused by a virus that is carried by a mosquito. The mosquito transports the virus from a wild bird or animal to your horse. The horse gets a high fever and then is paralyzed and dies within 2 to 4 days. A yearly vaccination will protect your horse.

Influenza

The common name for this disease is the "flu." It is caused by a virus. Many horses get the flu, but very few die from it. It is carried in the air. When one flu-infected horse coughs, another horse can breathe in the germs and get sick, just like your catching a cold at school. A horse with the flu has a fever, runny nose, and a cough. The flu can be treated by your veterinarian. The best bet is to vaccinate your horse once or twice a year, especially if there is a flu problem near where your horse lives.

Rhinopneumonitis

The common name for this disease is a "cold" or the "snots" because the infected horse has a lot of white discharge coming out of his nose. It usually affects foals that are 4 to 6 months old when they are weaned from their mothers. If a pregnant broodmare comes in contact with this virus, she could lose her baby (abort).

It is best to quarantine any horses that have rhino and vaccinate horses once or twice a year against the disease. Ask your veterinarian how many times you should vaccinate your horses against rhino. If your farm is at risk, the vet will probably encourage you to vaccinate at least twice a year.

Distemper

The common name for the disease is "strangles." It is a bacterial infection that causes the glands near the throat to swell and eventually rupture. The sick horse will not eat or drink and has a very high fever. A lot of very thick, yellow pus comes out of the horse's nose and the ruptured area at the throat. A horse rarely dies from strangles, but you will need to disinfect everything the horse comes in contact with because it is very contagious. Ask your veterinarian whether you should vaccinate against strangles.

Rabies

Rabies rarely affects horses, but when it does, it usually results in violent, dangerous behavior and death. The rabies virus is transmitted from an infected animal to the horse by a bite, usually from a dog, a skunk, a fox, or a bat. If rabies has been reported in your area, your veterinarian might suggest that you vaccinate your horse against the disease.

Equine Infectious Anemia

This is a deadly disease commonly called "swamp fever." It is a virus that lives in the horse's blood and is spread from one horse to another through a biting insect. There is no vaccine to protect your horse against swamp fever, but there is a test to see if your horse has been exposed to the disease and is a carrier. That test is called the Coggins test. A Coggins test is required if you are going to travel out of state with your horse or take him to a horse show or clinic. If a horse is found to be a carrier of equine infectious anemia, he might have to be put to sleep.

Preventing the Spread of Contagious Diseases

If you think there is a contagious disease at your place or at your neighbor's, or if you have been to a stable or horse show where there were sick horses, you will need to work closely with your veterinarian to bring it under control. You will need to use a combination of treatment, disinfecting, and quarantine to keep the disease from spreading and to get rid of the bacteria or virus that caused it.

Treatment usually means drugs that your veterinarian will give your horse. Disinfecting requires you to use a special medicated soap to scrub your horse's feeders, waterers, and living quarters to get rid of the microscopic "bugs" that caused the disease. Sunlight is a very powerful disinfectant, especially if the weather is hot and dry. Quarantine means keeping any horses that have been sick or seem to be getting sick separate from the healthy horses at your place.

Whether you have a disease problem or not, any new horse should be quarantined and observed for at least a week before you allow him to come in contact with your other horses or their eating or drinking areas. Any horse that leaves your place should be quarantined upon return, especially if it has been exposed to a large number of other horses, such as at a horse show.

Common Health Problems of Horses

If your horse gets sick or hurt, you should know enough about what is happening so that you can talk to your veterinarian on the phone and describe what you observe. If you make a daily health check such as I have suggested, you will notice if your horse is different one

Ways Disease and Infection are Usually Spread

- Directly from one horse to another horse

- From a contaminated stall or feeder to a horse

- Between horses eating or drinking from the same place

- Through the air

day and know that something is wrong. For example, if your horse is usually standing by his feeder in the morning when you come out to feed and one day you come out and he is lying down and doesn't get up when you put out his feed, you know something is wrong. I'll describe some of the most common problems that horses have. I hope your horse doesn't ever have any of them, but if he ever does, this information will make you better able to care for him.

Colic

Colic is similar to a stomachache. Something has upset your horse's digestive system.

Symptoms

If your horse is suffering from colic, he will probably either be very depressed or very restless. A restless horse lies down and gets right back up again, or lies down and rolls over and over, or kicks at his belly with his hind legs, or turns his head around and looks at his sides. A depressed horse just stands or lies without moving as if he has given up and just feels awful. He won't eat or drink at all. If your horse shows either of these types of symptoms, you'd better call your veterinarian. Have the answers to these questions ready if your veterinarian asks them:

Two types of colic symptoms. Top, the horse is restless and anxiously looks at his sides or bites them. Bottom, the horse is depressed and listless; he won't touch his feed or water.

- When did you first notice this?

- Has the horse had a change in feed?

- Has he been drinking water?

- Did you see any fresh manure piles in his pen or stall?

Treatment for Colic Until the Vet Arrives

After you have had a chance to talk with your veterinarian about your horse's condition, ask if you should walk your horse or not. In some cases of colic, it is helpful to walk the horse. The quiet exercise helps to move whatever feed is causing the problem through

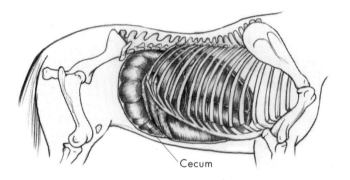

Cecum

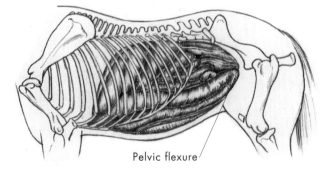

Pelvic flexure

(Top) The right side of the horse showing the cecum, where food can become impacted and cause colic. (Bottom) The left side of the horse showing the pelvic flexure, an abrupt turn in the intestines which is another place where feed can get stuck and cause colic.

the horse. Often your horse will poop or pass gas while you are walking him. When that happens, he will start feeling much better right away.

In other cases of colic, however, it is best **not** to walk the horse and to keep him very quiet. The better the information you provide your veterinarian, the better she will be able to tell you what to do until she gets there.

Lameness

Lameness is a problem that makes it difficult or painful for your horse to swing his legs forward or put weight on his feet.

Symptoms

Remember that when horses rest, their favorite position is standing on three legs. But if you find your horse limping or holding up a leg and not wanting to put any weight on it, he might be lame.

Treatment

If your horse is truly sore on one of his feet or legs, here are the things you should check.

First look for obvious wounds on any of the legs. Some wounds are very hard to see and unless you look very closely you will miss them. Puncture wounds are like that. If your horse ran into a stick and it poked a hole into his leg, the wound would be very small but it would be deep and there might even be some pieces of the stick deep in his leg. That's why you need to look carefully. If you find a wound, ask an experienced horseperson to look at it and decide whether you need to call the veterinarian.

Look at each hoof and pick it out, keeping your eyes open for rocks, wood splinters, nails, fence staples, wires, or anything else your horse could have picked up.

While you are looking at each hoof, examine the shoes to see if they are loose or have shifted in position.

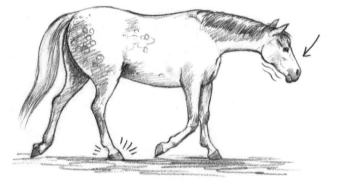

When the front leg is lame (top), when it lands, the horse raises his head to lift weight off the lame leg. When the hind leg is lame (bottom), when it lands, the horse lowers his head to shift the weight forward and off the lame leg.

One of the horseshoe nails might be causing a problem.

If you can't find a wound and picking out the hooves doesn't help, your horse should be examined by a veterinarian.

Cut or Other Injury

Any time your horse has been seriously injured, you should call your veterinarian immediately. When your horse has a large or deep wound, the quicker your veterinarian can close and treat the wound, the better

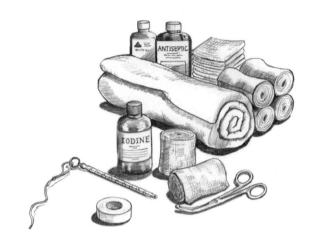

Horse first-aid kit

chance your horse will have of healing. Some very small wounds will not require your veterinarian's care. But you should ask your mentor's opinion on how to treat any wound.

Treatment

The best way to clean most wounds is to let water from a hose run over the wound for a few minutes.

Be sure the wound has been thoroughly cleaned before you apply any type of bandage.

Don't apply any home remedies, gook, or wound creams to a wound until an experienced horseperson or a veterinarian has looked at it.

Founder (Laminitis)

Founder is also called laminitis. It is a serious lameness of the hooves. Founder can be caused when a horse eats too much grain or green pasture, when a hot horse drinks cold water, or when a horse is ridden too long or fast on a hard surface, and can be caused by other circumstances.

Most wounds can be cleaned with water from a hose. Hold the hose above the wound and let a gentle stream of water flow over the wound for two minutes.

Symptoms

When a horse has founder, his hooves get very hot and painful and he has difficulty moving and standing.

Treatment

If your horse has the symptoms of founder, call your veterinarian immediately. The vet will prescribe treatment. Most horses that have foundered once will founder again and might always have lameness in their hooves.

Navicular Disease

Navicular disease is a painful condition of the front heels. It is caused by poor conformation of the hooves and legs, poor shoeing, lack of regular hoof care, or working a horse too hard or on poor footing.

Symptoms

A horse that has navicular disease takes short, shuffling, stiff steps.

Prevention and Treatment

The best way to prevent navicular disease is to find a good horseshoer and keep your horse on a regular shoeing schedule. Even if a horse already has navicular disease, special shoes can help him be comfortable and useful.

Thrush

Thrush is a disease of the *frog* area of the hoof. It is caused by wet, dirty stalls or pens. The filth lets a particular bacteria destroy the frog tissue.

Symptoms

If your horse has thrush, you will notice an awful smell when you pick out his hooves. There will be a black gook something like tar deep in the clefts of the frog.

Frog. *The thick, triangle-shaped tissue on the bottom of a horse's hoof. (See the illustration on page 80.)*

Treatment

If your horse has thrush, keep his hooves very clean and dry. Ask your farrier or veterinarian to treat your horse's hooves. The treatment might include a solution that you will apply a few times to help your horse's hooves heal faster.

Tying Up

Tying up is the common name for azoturia, a condition that usually occurs when a horse is fed too much grain and not exercised regularly.

Symptoms

When a horse ties up, his muscles cramp and it is painful for him to move. If, after a few days without exercise, a horse that has been on full feed is taken for a ride, in about 15 minutes his muscles could cramp up.

Treatment and Prevention

If your horse ties up, do not force him to move because it would probably tear his muscles. Send for help. Meanwhile, keep the horse quiet and warm. Put a blanket over his hindquarters. To prevent tying up, if you know you won't be riding your horse for a few days or more, decrease his grain ration.

Heaves

Heaves describes a disease of the lungs that usually occurs in horses over 5 years old. This condition might have originally been caused by an infection. But once the damage has been done to the lungs, the horse will always have the condition, even after the infection is gone. Exercise, dusty pens, a dry climate, and moldy or dusty hay will make it much worse.

Symptoms

A horse with heaves has a hard time breathing. He coughs and has to use his belly muscles to help his lungs breathe.

Treatment

There is no cure for heaves, but a horse with a mild case of heaves can be made more comfortable by wetting his hay down before feeding it to him and keeping him in a clean environment.

Preventing Poisoning

Horses like to investigate unknown things by nibbling and tasting. To be sure your horse cannot poison himself, keep all dangerous substances out of his reach.

Paint

Be sure the paint that is on your horse's fence and pen rails and on any building near him is safe. Paint that has lead in it can be very harmful to your horse if he swallows it.

Horse Products

Before you use **any** product on or near your horse, be sure you read the label very carefully. Make sure you don't accidentally give your horse an overdose of an antibiotic, dewormer, or nutritional supplement. Some dewormers (organophosphates) can be poisonous when they are used several times in a row because they can accumulate in a horse's body. That's why you should be sure you know what you are using when deworming.

Grain and Seeds

Don't feed your horse grain or seeds that are meant for planting because they might have been treated with mercury which will harm your horse. Treated grains often look pink or reddish, but sometimes they look exactly like the grain you normally feed your horse. So be extra sure!

Don't give your horse feed that is meant for cattle, sheep, or goats. These feeds often contain urea, a type of feed additive that is OK for ruminant animals (those with four-part stomachs) but not for horses, whose stomachs are very different. Also, some cattle feeds may contain growth stimulants that can permanently damage the nervous system of a horse.

Toxic Materials

Keep your horse away from junk or vehicles. Because horses use their lips to inspect things, they might eat poisonous paints, antifreeze, or battery fluid. Protect your horse from toxic fumes from vehicles, paints, and solvents. Don't apply insecticides or herbicides near feed or water areas and be aware of which way the wind is blowing when you are spraying.

Dental Care

Your horse should have a dental check up at least once a year.

Floating

If your horse is over 5 years old, probably all he will need is a *floating*. When the veterinarian or equine dentist floats your horse's teeth, she uses a large file to smooth the sharp edges of your horse's molars.

Young horses usually need to have their teeth floated every year, too. They also need two other checkups each year. Sometimes 2- and 3-year-old horses don't shed their baby teeth properly and the baby teeth get stuck on top of the adult teeth that are trying to push up. This makes it painful and difficult for your horse to chew. If your veterinarian looks at your horse's mouth, she can spot this problem and easily pop the baby "caps" off the adult teeth.

Wolf Teeth

Some horses have a small tooth, called a wolf tooth, in front of their molars. This tooth can cause problems if you use a snaffle bit on your horse because your horse's lip can get caught between the bit and the wolf tooth. You should have your horse checked for wolf teeth when he is about 1 year old. If wolf teeth are present, your veterinarian can remove them.

Hoof Care

A horse's hooves grow about ¼ inch per month and, like your fingernails, they must be trimmed regularly. If they are not trimmed regularly, they grow too long and break, causing serious damage. Most horses need professional hoof care every 6 to 8 weeks.

Be sure your horse has very good manners while having his feet handled and worked on so your farrier doesn't get hurt. Make sure you have a clean, level, dry place for your farrier to work that is out of the sun, wind, and rain.

Moisture Control

It is not good for your horse's hooves to be too wet. Mud and water cause the hooves to spread out like a pancake and split and break. Do not overflow your horse's water trough and make him stand in the mud. Hooves are healthiest when they are kept clean and dry and are trimmed regularly.

A liquid hoof sealer can help your horse's hooves by sealing out external moisture and sealing in moisture from the blood supply. Do not confuse greasy hoof dressing with hoof sealer. Hoof sealer is a thin, clear liquid that you paint on the hoof.

Daily Hoof Check

Every day before and after riding you need to check your horse's hooves for rocks, splinters, loose shoes, and loose nails. While you are checking, this is a perfect time to pick the hooves clean.

Cleanliness

Manure that becomes packed in a hoof makes a perfect home for bacteria and fungus that can cause the hoof to crumble and fall apart (see "thrush" on page 75).

Trimming should be done by an experienced horseshoer. If your horse stays barefoot, his hooves should be trimmed at least every 8 weeks.

Shoeing

If you are riding your horse a lot, he might need shoes to protect his hooves from too much wear. If your horse's hooves are crumbling or have cracks, he might need shoes to help hold his hoof walls together whether or not you are riding him. If your horse is wearing shoes, they should be checked by your horseshoer every 6 to 8 weeks.

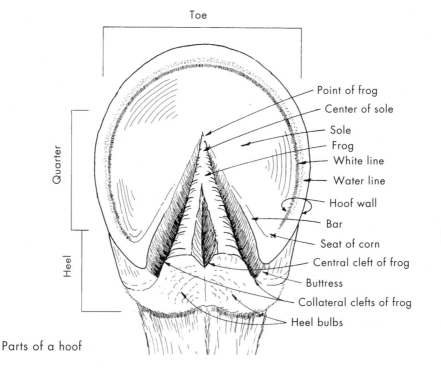

Toe

Quarter

Heel

Point of frog
Center of sole
Sole
Frog
White line
Water line
Hoof wall
Bar
Seat of corn
Central cleft of frog
Buttress
Collateral clefts of frog
Heel bulbs

Parts of a hoof

ILLUSTRATION: RICHARD KLIMESH

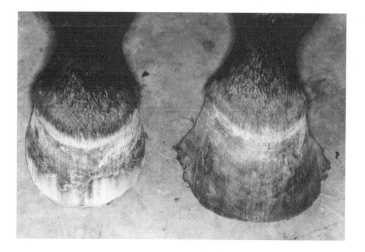

A hoof after trimming and a hoof that is way overdue for trimming. Your horse's hooves should never be neglected like the hoof at the right. This hoof has grown too long and is beginning to flare at the sides and break. Hooves should be trimmed or shod every 6 to 8 weeks.

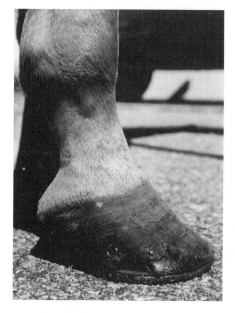

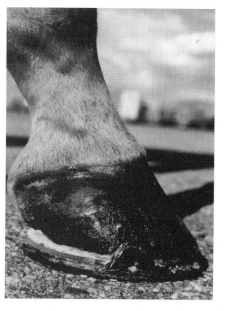

This hoof is way overdue for shoeing. The toe of the hoof is long and it has started to form a dish (a dip) at the toe. The shoe no longer supports the heels of the horse's hoof and the horse could suffer damage to his legs if he were ridden or exercised with these long hooves. Never let your horse's hooves get in this condition.

This is the same hoof after shoeing. Notice how the front wall of the hoof is straight, the hoof has been shortened, and the toe no longer has a dip in it. Now the shoe is placed directly under the heels where it should be to support the horse's leg.

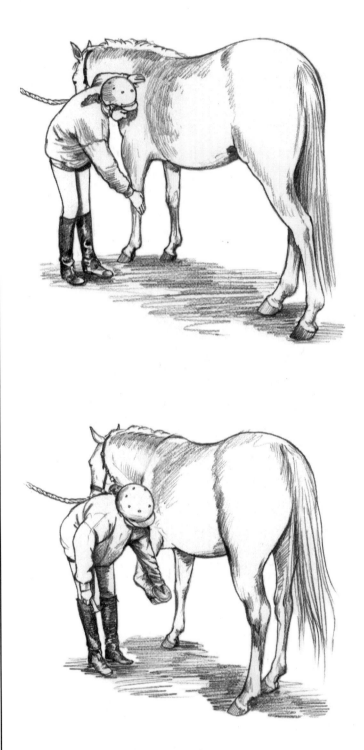

To pick up a left front foot, use your left hand on the horse's shoulder to shift his weight to his right leg. At the same time, run your right hand down the horse's left leg.

When he picks up his foot, catch it with your left hand. Hold the leg under the horse's body. Don't pull it out to the side. Take your hoof pick out of your pocket. You are ready to begin cleaning the hoof.

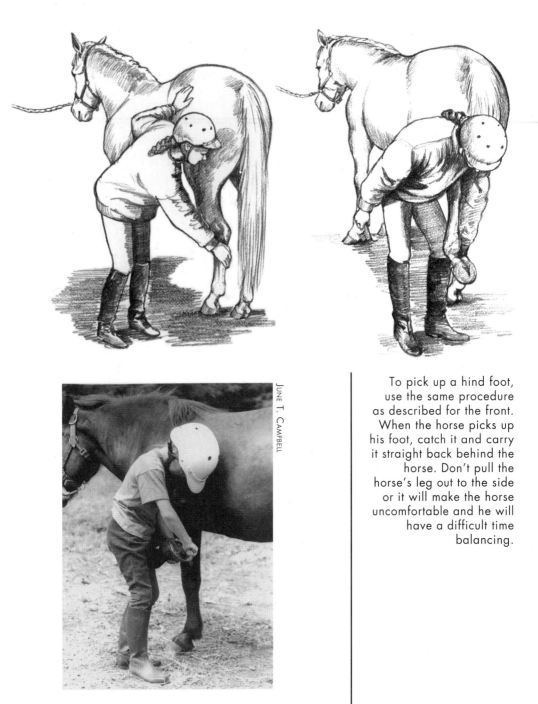

Cleaning a hoof can require hard work, especially if the sole is packed with mud, rocks, or snow.

To pick up a hind foot, use the same procedure as described for the front. When the horse picks up his foot, catch it and carry it straight back behind the horse. Don't pull the horse's leg out to the side or it will make the horse uncomfortable and he will have a difficult time balancing.

Exercise

Exercise is important for healthy hooves because when blood flows around your horse's body, his legs and hooves get their share. Fresh blood carries oxygen to the tissues of your horse's hooves and nourishes the hooves so they can stay healthy.

If your horse is forced to stand still in a stall or small pen, the blood flow to his legs is very slow and the blood in his legs and hooves is "old, tired" blood.

Sanitation

Sanitation is a big word for keeping things clean, clean, clean! The cleaner you keep your horse and his stall, pen, or pasture, the healthier he will be. Sanitation includes cleaning up manure, keeping the area around your horse's living quarters dry, and keeping flies and other pests to a minimum.

Removing Manure

Whether your horse lives in a pasture or a stable, he will produce up to 50 pounds of manure every day! If manure and urine build up for just a few days in an enclosed barn, they produce a smell and a gas (ammonia) that will burn your eyes and lungs . . . and your horse's! Also, if your horse is forced to stand in wet manure and urine, it will cause his hooves to break down. It can also cause him to suffer from a painful hoof condition called thrush (see page 75).

Since all manure contains worm eggs, you want to pick it up every day and get it away from your horse. Once you pick up the manure you have three choices:

After you clean your horse's stall or pen, you might want to sprinkle lime or a freshener over the wet spots to deodorize and sanitize the ground and help it to dry out.

1. You can have the manure hauled away. Some garbage collection services will carry manure away with your garbage.

2. You can spread the manure on a field or pasture that won't be used by horses during the year. It is best to spread the manure very thinly so that it is exposed to the sun and drying wind, which will kill the worm and fly eggs.

3. You can store the manure in a pile to spread later. When manure is stacked in a neat pile, it will compost or break down and turn into humus, a dark, fine, substance that has no odor. Humus is very valuable to add to the soil of your garden or flower beds or to spread on a pasture. It will take from two weeks to three months for a pile of manure to turn into humus, depending on your climate, rainfall, and the type of bedding that is mixed in with the manure. You will probably want to keep two manure piles going all the time. One is the old pile that is "cooking" or turning into humus. And the other is the fresh pile that you are adding to every day.

Flies

Stable flies, horseflies, deer flies, horn flies, and face flies are all blood suckers that can really cause problems for both you and your horse. The most common type of fly that will bother your horse is the stable fly, so I'll talk about stable flies the most.

Stable flies are about the same size as the common house fly. However, stable flies suck blood and house flies do not. Stable flies bite your horse until he bleeds and then the flies feed on the blood. They like to feed on a horse's lower legs, flanks, belly, under the jaw, and

Be Careful with Lime

Lime is a white powder you can buy at your feed store in 50-pound sacks. It helps to dry and deodorize stall floors. But be careful. If you breathe the powder as it puffs in the air, it can burn your nose and lungs. There are other products similar to lime that aren't as dangerous for you to handle. Ask at your feed store for other stall fresheners.

at the junction of the neck and the chest — all the places where your horse's skin is the thinnest and easiest for a fly to bite through. The bite from a stable fly is painful. Some horses panic when flies are after them and could run through a fence trying to get away from the flies. Even tough horses that try to put up with flies still spend the entire day stomping their legs to keep the flies from biting. This is very hard on their legs and joints and can cause the horse's shoes to become loose.

Stable flies lay their eggs in manure, wet hay, unclipped grassy areas, and other places where there is moist plant material. A female stable fly might lay twenty batches of eggs during her 30-day life span. Each batch contains between 40 and 80 eggs. It takes 21 to 25 days for the eggs to hatch. When the eggs hatch, the adult flies emerge ready to breed. (If you have seen tiny flies on manure and thought they were young stable flies, you were probably looking at a different type of fly.) The number of flies that can be produced by just one female is 1600 flies! If each of her 1600 kids had 1600 kids, that would make 2,560,000 flies! And that is just from one female fly to begin with!!

That's why the best way of controlling flies is to prevent them from breeding in the first place. Remove breeding grounds by picking up manure at least once a day. Keep your horse's living quarters dry. Be sure all pens and stalls drain well. Repair leaking faucets, hoses, and waterers. Dry out the wet spots in stalls and pens by clearing the wet bedding away, adding lime, and letting the ground dry out.

Even if you are the best horsekeeper in your state, you still will have a few flies to deal with. But you will have to use fewer fly sprays if you keep your facilities clean and dry. If you carelessly use insecticides to kill flies or repellents to keep flies from landing on your horse, you can cause harm to your horse, yourself, and the environment.

If necessary, you can use spray-on or wipe-on fly repellents when the flies are the worst. Ask your 4-H or Pony Club leader to help you decide what product to use. You can also attach fly shakers to your horse's bridle. Fly shakers are like fringe or extra bangs on your horse's forehead. These strips jiggle flies off your horse's face when he shakes his head. There are also several types of fly masks that your horse can wear that will prevent flies from landing around your horse's eyes. Also, your horse can wear a fly sheet, a cool, open-weave blanket that covers his body and prevents flies from getting at his skin.

During the worst of the fly season, you might want to get a fly mask for your horse to keep the flies from gathering around his eyes. Here are three different kinds.

Mouse Control

Sanitation also includes keeping the mouse population under control in your horse's living quarters. Rodents such as mice and rats can cause damage and health problems if they are allowed to breed and become too numerous in your barn area. Rodents can carry bubonic plague and rabies. They can also chew expensive *tack* and destroy it. If you let mice get started in your feed room, they will make a mess chewing through your feed sacks. All of your horse's feed should be stored in mouse-proof containers such as big garbage cans or bins. If you keep the grass around your barn trimmed and clean your barn regularly, you won't be providing good nesting sites for the mice. I don't recommend that you use poison and bait to kill rodents because it is too dangerous if you

If the flies are bothering your horse's body, you can get him a fly sheet that is made of a cool mesh that allows air to flow around your horse but keeps the flies off.

have cats, dogs, or younger brothers and sisters. I think having a few barn cats is much better than using poison. Cats are natural predators of mice and just the presence of a few cats in the barn will often keep mice away.

How to Clean a Stall or Pen

It is easier to clean a stall (or pen) when the horse is turned out for exercise. First remove the manure using a special fork that has tines close together. Then search for the spots of wet bedding and remove them. Push the dry bedding against the stall walls so the wet spots can dry. You can sprinkle a barn freshener or lime on the wet spots. Let the stall floor dry all day, if possible, with the barn doors and windows open.

Removing Manure

I prefer a metal silage fork because it will last longer, but you may prefer a light manure fork (sometimes called an "apple picker," because horse manure is sometimes jokingly called "road apples"!).

Stall cleaning tools: a fork for fluffing up clean straw; manure fork; aluminum scoop shovel; broom; muck bucket on wheels

When it is time to put your horse back into the stall or pen in the evening, rake the dry old bedding back to the area where your horse usually defecates and urinates. Add some new bedding, if necessary, to the place where your horse likes to lie down. Every week or so, you will need to remove all of the bedding from the stall. This is called "stripping the stall." You need to do this every so often and start fresh.

Before you return your horse to his stall, pick out his hooves and give him a good brushing. You don't want him to bring mud or manure into his freshly cleaned stall.

To clean your horse's stall or pen, use a special manure fork or a silage fork as shown here. The tines of the fork are close enough together so you can pick up the "horse apples" and leave the bedding behind.

This stall has been well cleaned. The manure and wet bedding have been removed and the clean bedding has been "banked" along the walls so the center of the stall can dry.

Grooming

CHAPTER 6

Grooming serves many purposes.

■ It cleans your horse's coat by removing dirt, sweat, dead skin cells, and loose hair.

■ It warms your horse up mentally by letting him get accustomed to your touch.

■ It warms your horse up physically because the rubbing and brushing increases his circulation (and if you are doing a good job, it should increase your circulation, too!).

■ It brings natural oils from the skin to the surface of your horse's hair to make his coat shine.

■ It lets you have a close-up look and feel of your horse's body to check him for nicks, bumps, or sore spots.

■ It helps you to train your horse to overall body handling so he doesn't have any ticklish areas.

Grooming Tools

Following is a list of the most common grooming tools and a description of what each is used for. You will want to get these tools for caring for your own horse.

Grooming Tools

- Hoof pick
- Rubber curry
- Dandy brush
- Body brush
- Cloth
- Sponge
- Sweat scraper
- Rubber grooming mitt
- Metal curry
- Mane and tail brush

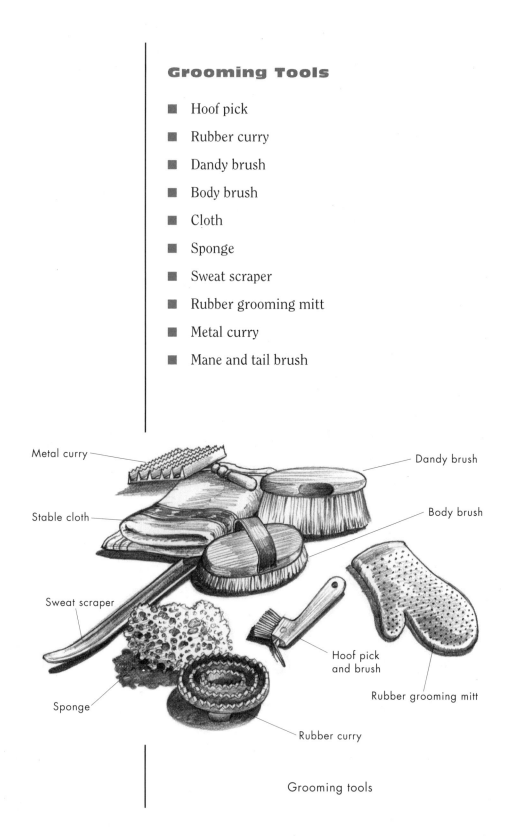

Metal curry

Stable cloth

Sweat scraper

Sponge

Dandy brush

Body brush

Hoof pick
and brush

Rubber grooming mitt

Rubber curry

Grooming tools

Hoof Pick

Use a hoof pick to remove mud, manure, stones, and splinters from the frog and sole of your horse's hooves. One type of hoof pick has a stiff bristle brush on the other side for removing mud from the hooves.

Rubber Curry

A soft or "gummy" rubber curry is great for loosening up mud and sweat on your horse's coat and for getting shedding hair to fall out. The soft rubber nubbins on the curry stimulate the skin to release hair oil to make a shiny coat. Use a curry in a vigorous circular motion. The rectangular type is easier for small hands to hold.

Rubber Grooming Mitt

The grooming mitt serves about the same purposes as the rubber curry but is used on sensitive areas such as your horse's legs and head. Put it on like a glove and then use your hand to conform to the part of the horse's body that you are working on.

Dandy Brush

A stiff-bristled dandy brush (sometimes also called a "mud" brush) removes the large pieces of dirt and hair that you brought to the surface of the coat with the rubber curry. The dandy brush is used with a short stroke and a flicking motion of your wrist. Rather than just push the dirt and old hair along the coat from front to back, you want to flick it off.

Metal Curry

The metal curry is not designed to be used on the horse's body. It is for keeping the bristles of your dandy brush clean. Hold the metal curry in your left hand while you are brushing with your right hand.

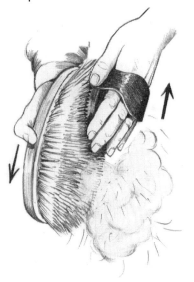

You can use a rubber or metal curry to help clean the bristles of the dandy brush.

Every time you make five strokes or so with the dandy brush in your right hand, run the bristles of the brush over the teeth of the metal curry to clean the bristles.

Body Brush

A body brush is a short, soft-bristled brush that further cleans the coat after the dandy has been used on the body and the rubber grooming mitt has been used on the head and legs.

Stable Cloth

Use a section of an old bath towel or a wash cloth, either damp or dry, to clean your horse's eyes, nostrils, anus, udder or sheath. It is also handy to keep your hands clean!

Mane and Tail Brush

Usually, you can pick through a horse's tail with your fingers. Sometimes it helps if you oil your hands a little (use one teaspoon of baby oil or a mane and tail product especially made for horses). When brushing is necessary, use a regular human hairbrush, not a comb. Combs cause too much hair to be pulled and broken. Begin brushing a tail or a long mane from the bottom and as you get the tangles out of the ends, you can work your way up.

Stable Rubber

A tightly woven cloth is used to remove any remaining dust from the coat and smooth the hair. Always wipe in the direction of hair growth to set the coat and give the finishing touch.

1.

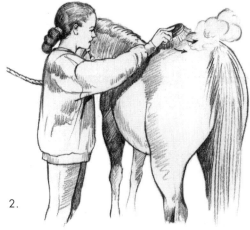

2.

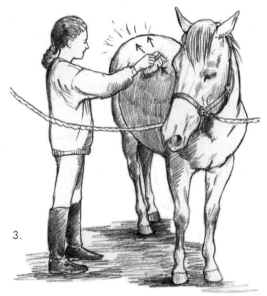

3.

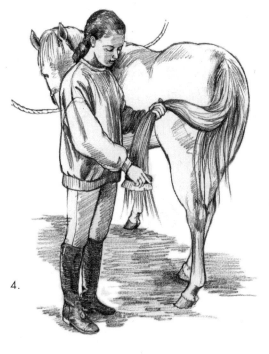

4.

5.

1) Use the rubber curry in a circular motion.
2) Use the dandy brush with a flick of the
wrist to send dirt flying. 3) Use the body
brush to finish the coat. 4) Stand to the side
when brushing out the tail. 5) Wipe the
head with a damp sponge or cloth.

Bathing

How Often to Bathe

A horse should be bathed often enough to keep him clean but not so frequently that his hair and skin become dry.

The horse's skin produces a valuable oil which repels water, lubricates the skin, keeps bacteria and fungus at a low level, and makes the coat shine. But the same oil also attracts dirt and causes it to stick to the coat. So you need to let the skin oil do its job, but you don't want it to become too heavy in your horse's coat. Too much bathing can remove a horse's natural protection and allow his skin to become dry and populated by harmful skin organisms. Frequent baths can also cause leg and hoof problems. (See Sanitation, Moisture Control in Chapter 5.)

Two or three baths a year is about right for most horses, including a late spring bath just after your horse has finished shedding; a mid-summer bath; and a fall bath just before your horse starts growing his winter coat but while the weather is still warm.

When to Bathe

Generally, it is safe to give your horse a bath when the temperature is above 50°F and you are able to bathe and dry your horse out of the wind.

If you are bathing a horse in preparation for a show or a photo session, bathe him the day before and keep him blanketed. A freshly shampooed coat "stares" — the hairs stick straight out from the horse's body. But after 24 hours under a blanket, the skin oil will make the hair lay flat and be shiny.

Where to Bathe

If you have a wash rack indoors, that is ideal. The floor of the wash rack should be texturized so the horse won't slip.

Equipment List for Bathing

- Clean halter
- Wool cooler
- Hose
- Hose brush
- Buckets
- Sponges
- Cloths
- Rubber mitt
- Leg brush
- Sweat scraper
- Large towels
- Shampoo solution
- Conditioner solution

If you will be bathing your horse outdoors, choose a place that won't get muddy; otherwise, it will be very hard to do a good job. A concrete pad or a rubber-matted area with a safe place to tie is best. Of course, it needs to be close to a water faucet.

Bathing Supplies and Equipment

On the day you plan to bathe your horse, prepare for the bath by getting your supplies and equipment ready.

Water

What you will need: If you do not have warm water in your barn, fill three or four 5-gallon buckets with cold water and set them out in the sun to warm for a few hours. Warm water is more pleasant for your horse and it does a better job of cleaning his coat because it dissolves oils and dirt more easily than cold water does.

Shampoo

Stick with a well-known horse shampoo. (Ask your instructor, someone at your farm supply store or tack shop, or another experienced horseperson to help you choose a good shampoo for your horse.) Dish detergent and laundry detergent are too harsh. They will dry out your horse's hair and could irritate his skin.

Dilute the shampoo according to the following directions. Take a large, clean plastic squeeze bottle (from ketchup or dish soap) and fill it with water up to about an inch from the top. Squeeze two good squirts of your horse's shampoo into this bottle of water. This is what you will use as shampoo for your horse. If you put straight shampoo on your horse, you will never be able to completely rinse the soap out of his coat.

To prepare for giving your horse a bath, get everything ready: Fill four or five buckets with water and set them out in the sun to warm. Gather your brushes, sponges, rubber mitts, sweat scraper, shampoo, and conditioner. Bathe your horse in a spot where a hose can easily reach.

If your horse's legs and head are very dirty, you will have to clip the fetlocks, throat, and bridle path after the horse has been bathed and is completely dry. Clipping dirty hair will make your clipper blades dull instantly!

Seven Steps of A Bath

1. Wet
2. Shampoo
3. Rinse
4. Condition
5. Rinse (if necessary)
6. Dry
7. Finish

Conditioner

Coat conditioners can contain substances that smooth the hair, moisturize it, add shine, and protect the coat from the sun. Your horse may benefit from a coat conditioner that contains a moisturizer and a sun screen. Ask for recommendations from an experienced horseperson.

Dilute your horse's coat conditioner in the following manner. Fill a small pail (1–2 gallons) with water. Add a few good squirts of conditioner to the pail and mix it in well. Pour the conditioner solution slowly over the horse's mane, hindquarters, and tail. You might need to mix up several buckets to finish your horse.

How to Give Your Horse a Bath

Before you bathe your horse you must groom him very thoroughly. Grooming loosens the dirt and moves it toward the surface of the hair where the shampoo has a better chance of carrying it away.

Unless the hair is very dirty, clip the fetlocks, throat, and bridle path before bathing.

If your horse is shedding, remove as much hair as possible before you start the bath.

Step 1: Wet the Horse

Get your horse used to the feel and the temperature of the water by slowly wetting his legs first. Start from the hoof and work your way up. Then wet his entire body, one section at a time. For this you can use a hose (if your horse is used to it) or a bucket and a sponge.

You might want to divide the horse up into sections and develop a routine for wetting, washing, rinsing, conditioning, and so on. Here's one way you could divide up your horse's parts into ten sections:

- Left shoulder from withers to knee

- Left side and back

- Left hindquarters to hock

- Right shoulder from withers to knee

- Right side and back

- Right hindquarters to hock

- Tail

- Left side of neck and mane

- Right side of neck

- Head

- Legs

Step 2: Shampoo the Horse

Now shampoo and rinse your horse one section at a time. For safety, start near shoulder so you can get your horse used to the idea before you tackle the more sensitive areas like the legs, head, and tail. Squirt some shampoo solution onto a section of your horse. Scrub, add more water, scrub.

When you are shampooing, don't skip these easy-to-forget areas:

- Throat area between your horse's jaw bones

- Area between your horse's front legs and just behind the elbows

- Area between the hind legs

- Belly

- Anus

- Sheath or udder

You might need help with some of these areas because unless you are very experienced and have a very gentle horse, you might have trouble getting the job done.

Step 3: Rinse the Shampoo Out of the Coat

Rinse the section you shampooed until no more soap-suds appear and until your horse's coat feels squeaky clean. If his hair is still slippery, he needs more rinsing. Use a sweat scraper to remove excess water.

Step 4: Condition the Coat

After all of the sections of the horse have been shampooed and rinsed, pour the conditioning solution all over your horse. (See page 98.)

Step 5: Rinse Out the Conditioner (if necessary)

Read the label of the conditioner carefully. If it says to rinse the conditioner out, then do so after about 5 minutes. If the label says to leave the conditioner on, then you can skip this step.

Step 6: Dry the Horse

Use a sweat scraper (or your hands) to remove all water from the heavily muscled areas of the shoulder, back, belly, and hindquarters. The more you remove with the sweat scraper, the faster your horse will dry. Buff his head and legs with dry towels. Put a wool cooler on him so that he won't get chilled as he is drying. You can let him stand tied somewhere as he dries or you can lead him. If you turn him loose in a pen or pasture, the first thing he will do is roll, so you want to keep him somewhere where he will stay clean until he is thoroughly dry and finished.

Step 7: Finish the Horse

Make sure all of the mane is lying on one side of your horse's neck. If it is not, place it there carefully with your fingers. Don't use a brush on your horse's mane until it is completely dry. Use a comb only **after** you have thoroughly brushed the dry mane. The same goes for the tail. Wait until it is completely dry. You will damage and break many tail hairs if you try to comb through it when it is wet. If you have a finishing spray for the mane and tail, apply it when the tail is just barely damp and work it in by drawing your fingers through the mane and tail.

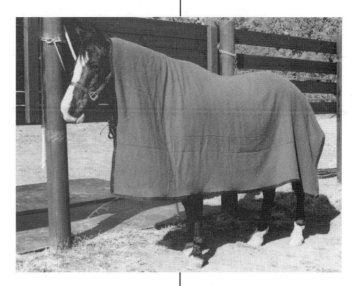

After your horse has been bathed and rinsed well and you have removed most of the water from his body with a sweat scraper, put a wool cooler on him and let him dry out in the wind.

Special Notes about the Mane and Tail

When you are shampooing the mane, don't just wash the hair. Scrub the crest of the neck, the 1-inch-wide strip that runs along the top of the horse's neck where the mane hair starts. Shampoo the crest really well and rinse it even better! If you do not keep this area clean and rinse the soap out thoroughly, it may start to itch. When your horse rubs against something to scratch the itch, he can rub his mane hair completely out in places.

The same goes for the dock of the tail. The dock is a long, thick, fleshy covering over the horse's tailbones at the top of the tail. All of the tail hairs grow from the dock. If the dock itches, a horse can rub his tail out when he scratches. Keep the dock very clean and well rinsed. Don't forget to clean the underside of the dock.

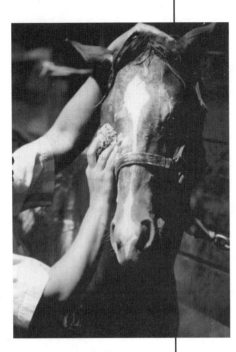

Special Notes about Shampooing Your Horse's Head

Wet and rinse a horse's head using sponges full of water rather than a hose. That way you can be more careful about not getting soap and water in your horse's eyes, ears, or nose. If you spray your horse's head with a hose, he will be afraid for the safety of his eyes and ears and he will learn to hate bathing.

To rinse your horse's head properly, hold a sponge full of water at his *forelock* and slowly squeeze, letting the water trickle down his face. Once your horse's head is rinsed really well, you can buff his head with a towel. He will love that.

Be very careful when you sponge your horse's head that you don't get soap or water in his eyes, ears, or nose.

Forelock. The tuft of hair that grows between a horse's ears and falls on the forehead.

Clipping

If your horse is not perfectly mannered about clipping, you will need someone to train him for you before you try to clip him yourself. He will need to get used to the sight and sound of the clippers and also their smell and the feel of the vibration of the clippers on his body.

While you are clipping, be sure the electric cord is out of the way so that neither you nor the horse becomes tangled in it. The clippers must have sharp blades. If the blades are dull, the clippers will pull on the horse's hair and cause him to dislike being clipped. Even if your horse is well trained about clipping, before you begin, let him see and smell the clippers. Rub the clippers on his neck with the motor turned off. Then turn them on. Turn them off and move the clippers to the bridle path area or to his legs, wherever you want to clip. Leave the clippers off and move them around the area as if you are clipping. Then turn the motor on.

How long of a bridle path do you want to clip? I suggest you clip a 2 to 3-inch bridle path which will give the halter and bridle a neat place to lay.

Clip all the long fetlock hairs from your horse's legs as this will help you keep his legs clean. Don't clip the hairs around the nose and eyes and inside the ears because these hairs protect your horse. Nature has provided face whiskers so your horse can put his head into a space that he can't see without getting hurt. The whiskers act like antennae to tell him when he is getting close to bumping into something. If you clip these whiskers off, he will lose his "second set of eyes." And if you remove the hair from inside his ears, tiny gnats and flies will be feasting in there in no time, which will be very painful for your horse and could make him *head shy,* which means he'll shy away when you try to touch his head. So, for your horse's good, when you are clipping, just tidy up the bridle path and legs.

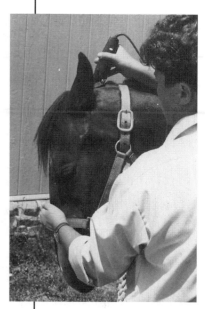

Before you try to clip your horse's bridle path, be sure he has very good manners for having his head handled. Ask your mentor to help you the first couple of times so you learn what to do.

Blanketing

If you will be keeping your horse in a stall a good deal of the time, you may need to invest in some stable clothing for him. A blanket is a replacement for a natural coat. It will inhibit the growth of a winter coat. If he has a winter coat, a blanket will cause him to shed earlier. Blanketing keeps your horse cleaner, too, so that grooming takes much less time. A blanket that is too light simply won't make much difference. A blanket that is too heavy is unhealthy because it may make the horse sweat and then get chilled.

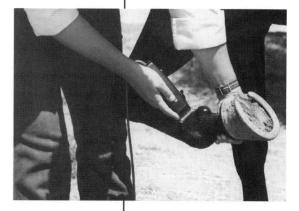

To be on the safe side, when you clip your horse's legs, pick them up and hold them as you clip.

A blanket must fit a horse properly. A poorly fitting blanket can cause rub marks and sore spots on your horse's withers, shoulder, chest, and hips. A blanket

that is too large will slip and twist. It can even slip so much that the horse can become dangerously tangled. To be sure you buy the correct size blanket, measure your horse from the center of his chest along one side of his body to the crease between his hind legs. The blanket lining should be a smooth material to prevent damage to hair, especially the shoulder area and the mane area nearest the withers.

If you blanket your horse, be on the lookout for overheating. If your horse is wearing a very warm winter blanket on a sunny, calm winter day, he can become dangerously hot. Also, a nonbreathable waterproof blanket can trap heat and sweat against a

This horse has had her neck, sides, and belly clipped for more efficient cooling out during and after winter work (see the evidence of the clipping pattern on her neck). Therefore, she needs to be blanketed to protect her from the cold. This quilted Cordura nylon blanket is toasty warm and tough.

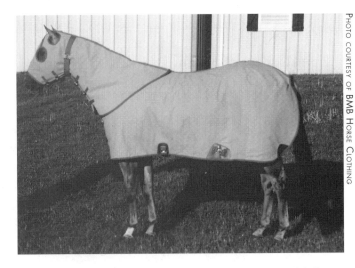

During the cool, wet weather of the spring and fall, you might want to use a lightweight waterproof blanket on your horse. If you plan to show your horse and have kept his coat short all winter, you might consider using a hood like this horse is wearing.

horse's body. If your horse is wearing a nonbreathable waterproof blanket and he overheats and sweats during the day, he will be cold and chilly at night and could get sick. When there is warm weather in the middle of winter, check to see if your horse is overheating and sweating by slipping your hand under his blanket at the heart girth area to feel for dampness.

A horse's blanket should be taken off and shaken out every day. Before you ride or exercise your horse, remove his blanket, turn it inside out, and hang it up. When you return, cool your horse out thoroughly, brush him, and put the blanket back on.

To determine blanket size, measure your horse from the center of his chest along one side of his body to the crease between his hind legs.

Types of Blankets

Sheet. A sheet is usually made of cotton. Cotton shrinks, so if you wash your horse's sheet in hot water, you will have to give it to your little sister's pony! A cotton sheet is light protection from dust, flies, and drafts. Use it as a protective cover during late spring, summer, or early fall.

Cooler. A cooler is usually made of wool, so you will need to wash it by hand in cold water. A cooler is usually draped loosely over a horse after a bath or exercise while he is cooling out or drying off.

Fly sheet. This is a mesh sheet that lets air in but keeps flies out. It is used in summer so the horse does not get hot but flies stay off his body. Also called a scrim sheet.

Winter blanket. Many types of winter blankets are

available. Most are designed to be used in a barn because they are not weather proof. A winter blanket might be made of canvas with wool lining, which must be hosed with cold water and scrubbed by hand. Other winter blankets are made of quilted material, like a winter jacket. This type of blanket is machine-washable, but it requires a very large machine like the large-capacity washers at the laundromat. A winter blanket usually has two belly straps, a chest strap, and, sometimes, hind leg straps. You can usually get a matching hood that covers your horse's head and neck.

Turn-out rug or blanket (such as a "New Zealand Rug"). This type of blanket might be made of waterproof heavy canvas with a wool lining, or other weather-proof materials. It is rugged and tough and can be worn by a horse that lives outside for the winter.

Blanket Care

A blanket must be kept clean. A dirty blanket will cause your horse discomfort and may cause disease. If you keep the horse clean, the blanket will usually stay clean on the inside. If you let mud and manure build up on the outside of the blanket, the extra weight may be uncomfortable for your horse and may cause the blanket to shift to one side. Dirt and manure can also rot the blanket material. Keep the outside of the blanket clean by brushing, shaking, and even hosing the blanket. It will also be necessary to wash your horse's blanket. If your horse lives outside and rolls on the ground, you might need to wash his blanket every two or three weeks. If your horse and his stall are very clean, perhaps you will only need to wash the blanket once or twice a year.

Check the blanket regularly for loose stitching or straps that are frayed or cracked. Have the necessary repairs made before tears become so big that the blanket is ruined and no longer worth mending.

Safe Handling and Riding

Handling horses can be dangerous. But if you follow simple safety rules, you will have a much smaller chance of getting hurt. To be safe when you are handling or riding your horse, start with a safe attitude, dress properly, use safe equipment, and use sensible horse-handling methods.

Safe Attitude

You must have a safe attitude whenever you are around horses. The best way to develop a safe attitude is to watch very good horsemen and horsewomen as they work with horses. Ask your instructor or club leader to explain why things are done a certain way with horses. The better you understand these things, the easier it will be for you to become an accomplished horse handler and rider.

Working with horses and riding is a great privilege. Riding correctly and safely is your responsibility.

Following are the most common causes of accidents with horses, with examples of each.

Being careless when performing everyday chores; taking shortcuts. Example: You are bathing your horse and don't want to take the time to wet his head with a sponge so you spray his head with a hose and get water in his eyes and ears. He rears up and lands on you with his front feet.

Not having enough experience to handle a particular horse. Example: You go out to the pasture to catch a horse in a group. The horse keeps away from you by standing in the middle of the group of other horses. Every time you try to walk up to him, he turns his rump toward you. The other horses are milling around and you are kicked or stepped on.

Losing your temper. Example: You are riding your horse and you are having difficulty stopping him. You pull harder and harder on the reins and start jerking on the bit and kicking the horse in his sides and say, "You stupid horse!" The horse rears up and falls over backwards on top of you.

Not having a good teacher. Example: Your instructor lets you take lessons without a safety helmet. You fall and suffer a concussion.

Not following a good teacher's advice. Example: Your instructor tells you never to ride your horse into the barn but you think it would be fun and do it anyway. You hit your head on the doorway.

Showing off or being silly. Example: You are showing your friend how quiet and sweet old "Buck" is by wrapping his lead rope around your waist. All of a sudden, some nose bots fly up Buck's nose. He snorts, rears, and takes off, dragging you behind, tangled in the rope.

Using unsafe equipment. Example: You tie a horse up with a weak, old halter and while you are cleaning his hoof, the horse leans backward, breaks the halter, and lands on top of you.

Working with a horse that has bad habits. Example: You are mounting a horse that doesn't stand still. He takes off when your left foot is in the stirrup but before you have swung into the saddle. You are dragged.

Working in an unsafe area. Example: You are riding

in a pen with a barbed wire fence. A small, yapping dog runs into the pen and nips at your horse's heels. Your horse panics and runs into the wire fence. You and your horse are severely cut.

Working with a young or untrained horse. Example: You are riding a 3-year-old that has been startled by a trainer and ridden for one month. The young horse is confused by your rein signals. You hold on tight and the horse starts bucking. You are thrown off and break your arm.

Not being able to read a horse's "body language." Example: When you try to catch your horse, you reach for his nose. He turns away, swings his hindquarters toward you, and steps on your foot. Your horse was trying to tell you that he would prefer to be touched on his neck or withers.

Bad luck (the horse slips or falls). Example: It is a muddy day and you are trotting your horse down a small hill that is normally safe to trot or canter down. Your horse loses his footing and balance, and he falls.

Safe Clothing

Proper clothing is an important part of safe handling and safe riding.

Footwear

Always wear hard-toed boots or shoes when you are working around your horse. If you wear soft shoes or sandals and your horse accidentally steps on your foot, your toes could be hurt very seriously. Also, be sure that your boots or shoes have soles and heels that give you good grip on the ground. If you wear slippery shoes around your horse, you can lose your footing and slide underneath him, which puts you in a very dangerous position.

Gloves

Because you must hold onto a lead rope when handling your horse, you should get used to wearing gloves when you are working with your horse. If your horse suddenly darts to the side and the lead rope "zings" through your hand, it can leave a nasty rope burn. The heat from the friction of the rope moving so fast against your skin is as painful as a burn from a hot stove. Gloves will protect you in such a case.

Helmet

Wear a safety helmet whenever you ride or work around horses. A helmet protects your head if you fall, if a horse bumps into you, or if a horse hits you with a hoof. Don't think that a safety helmet is only necessary for jumping. You should wear one for all types of riding and also when you are handling a horse from the ground.

If you are going to show, you will need to check the rules of the association governing the show to see what type of helmet is required.

You can buy many types of helmets, including those that look like Western hats. Not all helmets are constructed to absorb the concussion from a fall. Helmets approved by the Pony Club, AHSA (American Horse Shows Association), or USCTA (United States Combined Training Association) are labeled ASTM/SEI to show they have passed strict tests that prove they will protect your head.

Be careful when buying a used helmet because you won't know if the helmet has been damaged in an accident. A used helmet may look perfectly fine even though the inside protective layer has been damaged and won't protect your head in case of a fall.

Ask your instructor to help you choose a safe, approved helmet, and then wear it when you are handling or riding horses.

Rope Safety

Never wrap or loop a rope around your hand, arm, or other part of your body thinking it will help you hold onto your horse better. I have seen children get seriously hurt because they wrapped the rope around themselves and couldn't let go.

Safe Equipment

Use tack and equipment of the strongest type and inspect it regularly for wear. Tack should be well stitched, and constructed from durable materials. Choose a well-made nylon wide-web halter for everyday leading and tying. Use a ⅝-inch or ¾-inch-thick cotton lead rope with a sturdy snap on it.

Be sure your tack is not so old and worn out from dirt, sweat, rain, hot sun, or longtime use that it is no longer safe. When choosing tack, be aware that some tack is made to be very colorful and attractive but it might not be the strongest and safest tack to use.

Safe Facilities

Your training facilities should also be strong and safe. The place where you tie your horse needs to be very stout. It is best to tie your horse to the post of a specially designed tie area. If you tie to a rail or board, your horse could pull back, break the board, injure himself and others, and possibly panic, dragging the board along with him. If this happens to your horse only once, he will always be very suspicious every time he is tied.

Your training pens and arena should be at least 6 feet tall and very strong. When you longe or ride a horse in a training area, you want to be sure he can't get away.

Safe Horse-Handling Methods

Learn these safety tips and follow them whenever you are working with a horse.

Safe clothing includes a good helmet, gloves, and boots or shoes with hard toes.

Don't approach a horse directly from the front. Instead, approach from the side while speaking to him. Touch him on the neck, shoulder, or withers.

When approaching a horse from the rear, speak to him so he knows where you are and is not startled. Then touch him with the flat of your hand on the hindquarters as you move toward his head.

Approaching a Horse

- Always speak to a horse as you are approaching him.

- Approach a horse at an angle, aiming for the horse's shoulder. Never approach a horse by aiming directly at his head or his tail. Remember his "blind" spots.

- Touch a horse first by placing a hand on his shoulder or neck.

- Don't pet the end of a horse's nose. Doing so might cause him to move away or it might encourage him to nibble.

- Either walk around a horse well out of kicking range or move around the horse staying very close, with your hand on his hindquarters to let him know you are there. Never walk under or step over the tie rope.

Handling a Horse

- Know your horse.

- When handling a horse, protect your head by wearing protective head gear.

- Let the horse know that you are firm but will treat him fairly.

- Control your temper.

- Don't surprise a horse. Let him know what you intend to do by talking to him and touching him firmly. (Soft, feathery touches make a horse's skin twitch and cause him to move away.)

- Learn simple means of control from a knowledgeable horseperson and use them to control your horse when he becomes frightened or unruly.

- Stand near the shoulder rather than in front of the horse when clipping and braiding.

- Stand next to the hindquarters rather than directly behind a horse when working on his tail.

- Be calm and keep your balance.

- Do not drop tools or tack underfoot.

- Do not leave a halter on a loose horse. The horse may hook it on a post or a tree when rubbing or on his own hind shoe when scratching his head with his hoof.

- When working in an enclosed space, always take the time to plan an escape route in the event of an emergency.

Safe Haltering Procedure

Use proper haltering procedures to develop good habits in your horse and to avoid accidents. Approaching the horse from the near (left) side, hold the unbuckled halter and rope in your left hand. With your right hand, scratch the horse on the withers and move your

To halter a horse, first loop the lead rope around his neck so you have control of him as you work.

While you hold the rope loop at the top of the horse's neck, hand the halter strap to your right hand.

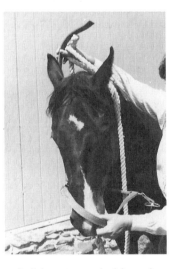

Still keeping a hold on the rope, place the halter on the horse's face.

right hand across the top of the neck to the right side. Use your left hand to give the end of the lead rope to your right hand. Make a loop around the horse's throatlatch and hold the loop with your right hand. If the horse tries to pull away at this stage, you can pull the horse's head toward you while pressing your right elbow into his neck. Next, hand the halter strap with the holes in it under the horse's neck to your right hand which is holding the lead rope loop. With your left hand, position the noseband of the halter on the horse's face and then bring your hands together at the poll to buckle the halter.

Leading a Horse

When leading a horse, always make the horse walk beside you. You should be next to his neck or shoulder. He should not lag behind or pull you ahead.

Turn the horse to the right (away from you) and walk around him rather than having him walk around you. This is the safest way to turn. Once you know your horse, you will want to be able to turn him the other way also.

Work your horse from both the right and left sides so that he develops suppleness and obedience each way and does not become one-sided.

Use an 8- to 10-foot lead rope. When leading from the left, with your right hand, hold the lead rope three to four inches from the snap that is attached to the halter. With your left hand, hold the balance of the rope in a safe configuration such as a figure eight. If you hold the lead rope in a coil in your left hand and your horse suddenly pulls, the rope might tighten around your left hand which can become trapped in the coil. Use your right elbow in the horse's neck to keep him straight and to prevent him from crowding you.

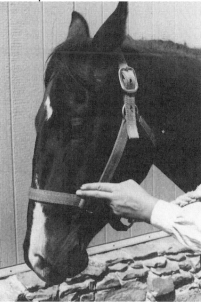

A halter fits properly when the noseband is two fingers below the prominent cheekbone.

If a horse resists or balks when you try to lead him, do not get in front and try to pull. Instead, stay in the proper position at the shoulder and urge the horse forward with a light tap from a long whip held in your left hand.

Never wrap a rope or strap around your hand, arm, or other part of your body. If a horse spooks suddenly and bolts, you may be unable to free yourself and could be hurt badly.

Teach your horse patience when turning him loose. Do not let him bolt away. If he forms this bad habit, he may pull away before you have the halter fully removed and you and he could become entangled. To turn your horse loose, follow the haltering procedure shown earlier in reverse. The loop is applied around the horse's neck, the halter is removed, and then the loop is released. Hold the horse momentarily with the loop and then gently push him away from you with your right elbow.

When you lead your horse, make him walk next to you. You should be next to his neck or shoulder.

When you turn your horse, turn him away from you and walk around him.

Tying a Horse

When you need to tie your horse, be sure he is wearing a strong nylon halter and that the lead rope and snap are heavy duty.

- Know how to tie the quick release manger knot without hesitation.

- Keep your fingers out of loops when tying knots.

- Be sure a horse is well accustomed to being tied in other ways before attempting to tie him in a *cross-tie*.

- Cross-tie. A means of tying a horse across an alleyway. A chain or rope from each side of the aisle attaches to the side rings of the halter.

- Tie horses a safe distance from each other.

- Never tie a horse with bridle reins. It would be far too easy for the reins to snap, which may cause damage to the horse's mouth and the potential for developing the bad habit of pulling when tied.

- Always tie at the level of the withers or higher.

- Always tie to a strong post or tie ring, not a rail that may be pulled loose.

- Untie a horse and hold him temporarily with the lead before removing the halter. Never remove the halter while the rope is still tied to the post. These two practices will help prevent your horse from developing the bad habit of pulling away.

a.

c.

b.

a) How to tie a quick release knot. b) The finished knot. If you pull on the tail, the knot will come undone. c) To keep a horse from turning himself loose by biting the tail and releasing the knot, you will have to drop the tail of the rope through the loop.

A horse on cross-ties in a grooming stall at a public stable

Bridling a Horse

In order to keep control of the horse while bridling, untie the lead rope from the hitching post, remove the halter from the horse's head, and refasten the halter around his neck. Hold onto the lead rope as you bridle.

Good bridling methods are similar to good haltering methods. Hold the crown piece of the bridle with your right hand. Drape the reins over your left arm. Hold the bit with your left hand. Present the bridle to the horse by moving your hands from the left side of his face to in front of his face. Hold your right hand in the area of his forehead while you move the bit into position between his upper and lower teeth. When the horse opens his mouth, gently place the bit between his teeth. Pull gently upward toward the horse's ears with your right hand. Then use your left hand to help put the horse's right ear into the bridle, then his left ear. Check for adjustment. Fasten the throatlatch and noseband.

To bridle a horse, follow the directions to the right. This handler is wearing a safety helmet, but she has let the reins dangle on the ground, which is dangerous.

Saddling a Horse

Be sure your horse is well groomed for saddling. Check the horse, the saddle, and the blanket for foreign objects such as burrs, hay, and dirt.

Place the blanket in front of the withers and slide it back into position. (If you place the blanket so that you must slide it forward into position, you will ruffle the horses' hair and that will be uncomfortable for him.)

Place the saddle on the blanket. Peak the blanket up in the gullet of the saddle so the blanket won't put pressure on the horse's withers. With a Western saddle, fasten the front cinch first, then the back cinch, then the breast collar and accessories. Reverse the order when unsaddling. The reason for this is that if a horse spooks with just a rear cinch fastened, the saddle could slip under his belly. This could cause him to buck, resulting in possible injury to himself and damage to the saddle.

Buckle the rear cinch so that it is snug but not tight. With an English saddle, attach the breast collar and accessories to the girth, then buckle the girth. Reverse the order when unsaddling. Tighten cinches and girths gradually. Check several times before mounting and after riding a short while.

Riding a Horse

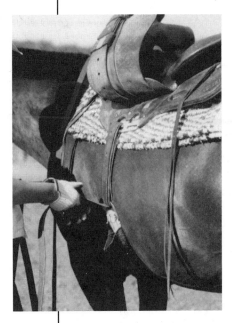

A cinch should be tightened gradually. With a Western saddle, always tighten the front cinch before the back cinch. This Western saddle does not have a back cinch.

Riding a horse requires good instruction and close supervision. There are many safety considerations. Here are a few:

■ Wear a protective helmet with full harness whenever you are riding.

■ Never mount where there is low overhead clearance such as under a building or tree.

■ When mounting, maintain control of the horse through light contact with the reins.

■ Confine your riding to an enclosed area until you know your horse.

■ Remain calm if your horse is frightened. Give him time to overcome his fear.

■ Never fool around when riding.

■ Don't rush past riders moving at slower gaits.

■ Don't allow your horse to approach and sniff a strange horse because what might happen next is squealing, striking, or kicking.

■ When riding with other horses in an arena, don't crowd them.

■ When you need to pass a horse that is going in the same direction as you are, move off the rail several horse lengths behind the horse and then make sure there is plenty of room between you as you pass. When you are several horse lengths in front of the horse you've just passed, you can go back to the rail.

■ Keep all equipment in good repair. Your safety depends on it.

Enjoying Your Horse

You can enjoy your horse or pony in many ways with your family and friends or with a youth group. First you should master the care of your horse. Then you should devote a lot of time to learning how to ride properly.

Only after you have become a well-rounded horse-person should you consider showing. The purpose of showing is to allow a good rider to demonstrate the thoroughness of his or her horse care and training abilities. You should be experienced and your horse well-trained before you step into the show ring. Then you will have a safe and enjoyable experience. Showing requires a lot of at-home preparation — not just a quick bath the day before the show but careful planning and training for months ahead of time.

Some youth groups teach you about horse care and horsemanship as well as competition skills. Remember, when you participate in a group activity, don't be a show-off with your horse. That usually leads to someone getting hurt. If you are entered in a show, no matter how small or large, do your best and hope to

Very young riders can show in lead line classes, where their horse is led by an adult.

win, but if you lose, be sure to grin. Congratulate the winner and think about what you need to work on to do a better job next time. Put fun before winning.

If you have family members or friends who are also interested in horses, you can find many ways to enjoy your horses together. Pleasure trail riding is one of the most satisfying and relaxing ways to use a horse. It can also be exciting, depending on where you go to ride. It is great fun to plan a day of trail riding with some friends and to meet at a park or trail area. If you can't easily get to a park or trail, you can plan get-togethers riding through pastures, along safe roadways, and in various arenas. Many of these activities are best enjoyed with an organized group. Look for flyers in your tack and feed stores for the names of local horseperson's groups. Call up the group's president or secretary and find out when and where the next meeting will be held. Attend the meeting as a visitor and see if the group has the same horse interests you do.

Participating in 4-H

4-H is a program run by the state or province in which you live. The 4-H covers all sorts of agricultural and livestock interests. The horse project is just one of them. 4-H has been in existence since the early 1900s.

The purposes of 4-H horse projects include:

■ To teach members how to confidently and safely care for and work with their horses using written materials and clinics.

■ To teach members skills involved in horseback riding.

■ To teach members safe ways of riding and handling horses to prevent injury to members or their horses.

■ To provide an opportunity for members to use their horses in a fun way, games, schooling shows, clinics.

- To help members develop leadership skills by organizing activities and by being an officer of a group.

- To work on community projects such as assisting in putting on a horse show or providing volunteer work for charities and fund-raisers (car wash, tack sale) that benefit equine research.

- To develop sportsmanship.

Usually a 4-H group is made up of between three and thirty kids and one or two volunteer leaders. The leaders are usually parents and they may or may not have horse experience. The group picks a club name that usually includes the name of the city or county nearby. Examples are the Harrison Hoofers or the Tyler County Trotters. The local club usually meets at least once every month and more often in the spring, summer, and fall.

The group meetings vary. Usually club business is taken care of before the program begins. Sometimes the program is a presentation by a member, such as a talk on bits. The member who gives the talk might bring a group of bits to show as he talks or he might make a chart of the parts of a bit. During the winter months, the program might include a talk from a local veterinarian or horse trainer.

Many of the programs involve riding and using your horse. You will need to trailer your horse to the meeting site. At the meeting site your leader or a guest instructor will explain the things that will be demonstrated and practiced that day. This usually lasts about 5 to 10 minutes. Then the instructor will use a horse and demonstrate how to do the things you will try later with your horse. This might take 10 to 20 minutes. During this time you should not talk with your friends. Instead, pay very close attention to what the instructor is doing because soon you will be trying the techniques on your own horse. Once the demonstration is over,

The 4-H Club Pledge

I pledge
My Head to Clearer
  thinking
My Heart to Greater
  loyalty
My Hands to Larger
  service
My Health to Better
  living
For My Club
My Community
My Country and my
  world

you will be asked to get your horse ready. Your leader and the guest instructor will help you and the other club members practice what you observed. In almost all cases, the guest instructor volunteers his or her time. He or she is giving time to your 4-H club so you should show your appreciation by paying attention and working hard.

This young rider very capably rides a well-trained Quarter Horse gelding in her hunt seat lesson. Notice her safe riding attire.

4-H Record Book

Creating the 4-H Record Book is a requirement for the horse project. In it, you must include:

- A description of your horse
- Pictures of your horse from all angles
- Drawings of your horse showing all markings and brands
- Your goals and how you plan to reach them
- Your horse's health and soundness history

- A description of all of your tack and equipment

- Feed records, including how much, what, and when you feed

- Veterinary records, including deworming, vaccinations, and other

- Farrier records

- Costs of all feed, bedding, veterinary care, hoof care, and tack

- Income you receive for prizes and sale of horses

- A record of regular meetings attended and what was covered in the program or clinic

- A record of special events you participated in, such as shows, tours, trail rides, field trips, and community services

- A record of your daily riding, including what you worked on and how long you rode

4-H Advancement Levels

4-H advancement levels is a systematic program for you to progress from a beginner to a more experienced horseperson. Usually there are 3 or 4 levels you can go through. Each level requires you to:

- Pass written tests

- Demonstrate specific handling and riding skills

- Give talks and demonstrations to your group

- Design and present projects

- Keep your record book and workbook complete at all times.

Everyone must begin with Level 1, the novice or beginner level. You must pass everything in that level to progress to the next level. You will be provided with a workbook so you can keep track of the things you have passed and what you need to work on. When you feel you are ready to pass a particular skill or a written exam, you make an appointment to be examined by a certified 4-H examiner. This will not be your regular 4-H leader. If you pass the test, the examiner will write her name and the date you passed in your workbook. It might take you one or two years to pass from one level into the next.

The 4-H Horse Show

Most counties and states have at least one 4-H show each year. If you are in a very horsey area, you might find that there is a 4-H show within 40 miles of your house every weekend of the summer. In the fall, there will be a big 4-H show at the county fair. Depending on how many 4-H members there are in your county, your shows might have just two classes or as many as twenty or thirty! I've listed some of the most common classes below. I suggest you read my book *From the Center of the Ring,* which describes all of the events in horse competitions in more detail (see "Recommended Reading" on page 139).

Showmanship

Showmanship is an *in-hand class* that judges your ability to exhibit your horse to a judge at halter. You will be showing your horse by leading him in a particular pattern that the judge will describe the day of the show. For this class, the quality of the horse does not matter. You do not need an expensive or fancy horse, but the horse must be very well cared for. He must be groomed like a million-dollar horse. He should be fit, healthy, clean, shiny, and have well-trimmed or shod hooves. The horse must have excellent manners and training while being led. The judge will be watching how well you and your horse work together.

Western Horsemanship

Western horsemanship is a riding class using Western tack and attire. It is a class where you demonstrate your skills as a Western rider. The quality of the horse is not being judged, but how well you and your horse work together is being judged. You will have to walk, trot, and lope in a group with the other contestants in the class. Then each of you will have to perform a special pattern alone that demonstrates your ability to control the horse without other horses nearby.

In a showmanship class, the exhibitor's horse must be in excellent health, very well-groomed, and well-mannered. This young exhibitor has done a nice job of preparing and setting his horse up for the judge's inspection.

Although winning ribbons is exciting, having fun and being a good sport are the most important parts of horse shows.

English Equitation

English equitation is a riding class using English tack and attire. It is a class where you demonstrate your skills as an English rider. The quality of the horse is not being judged, but how well you and your horse work together is being judged. You will have to walk, trot, and canter your horse in a group with the other contestants in the class. Then each of you will have to perform a special pattern alone that demonstrates your ability to control the horse without other horses nearby.

Other Classes

4-H shows might also have halter classes, gymkhana (barrel racing, pole bending, etc.), Western pleasure, hunter under saddle, and other classes.

Participating in Pony Club

The United States Pony Club (USPC) was established in 1954. There are over 500 clubs and 12,000 members. The word *pony* does not mean that all members own ponies. In fact, most members own horses.

The USPC was designed to teach (English) riding, mounted sports, and the care of horses and ponies to those under 21 years of age. USPC also provides opportunities for competition in various horse sports.

The mission of the USPC is to provide a program that also develops responsibility, moral judgment, leadership, and self-confidence.

Safety

Safety is an important part of participating in the USPC and is stressed in their guidelines. Clothing required for any horse sport must be neat, clean, and in good repair. Long hair must always be neatly

4-H Information

For more information on your local 4-H Horse Program, contact your county Extension office. In the business listing or government listing section (not the yellow pages) of your phone book, look under the name of your county. It will say something like: **Larimer County of** Cooperative Extension Service Office Agriculture, 4-H/Youth 498-7400.
It may also be listed under 4-H.

Part of the training of a rider should include lessons on the longe line, as this 15-year-old rider demonstrates. Her instructor controls the horse while the rider learns balance and develops her seat without using stirrups or the reins.

USPC is an educational organization which progressively develops the well-rounded horse-person.

The well-rounded horseperson is capable of riding safely and tactfully on the flat, over fences, and in the open.

Knowledgeable care of horses and ponies (horse management) is basic to the well-rounded horseperson.

USPC is committed to the well-being of the horse.

Fair and friendly competitions develop teamwork and sports-manship.

Fun and friendship are part of Pony Club.

USPC requires parental and volunteer involvement and support.

The USPC is committed to safety.

The local club is the core of USPC.

secured away from the rider's eyes. It is dangerous to wear hooped earrings and loose necklaces. Rings and bracelets are inappropriate and can cause injury if the rider falls.

When mounted, all Pony Clubbers must wear securely fastened helmets which meet current ASTM-SEI standards. The helmet must be worn so that the brim shades the eyes, not worn on the back of the head.

When riding, a conventional type of riding footwear with a heel, such as leather or rubber riding boots, jodhpur boots, or the equivalent is required. Waffle-type soles are not allowed. When dismounted, including when working around horses and in the barn, acceptable footwear is a shoe that is securely fastened, entirely closed, covers the ankle and is thick-soled and in good condition. Canvas or cloth shoes are not allowed. A Safety Information Packet is available from the USPC National Office.

USPC Competitions

USPC competitions include a variety of local, regional, and national competitions. Members can compete as individuals and as members of a team. The purposes of USPC competitions include:

- To provide members with an introduction to various horse sports.

- To provide members an opportunity to demonstrate the knowledge and skills they acquired through the USPC teaching program.

- To provide members an opportunity to demonstrate their ability to care for their mounts in a safe and workmanlike manner with minimal adult assistance.

- To provide members with opportunities to learn from other Pony Clubbers.

- To provide members with opportunities to develop responsibility, leadership skills, and sportsmanship through team experiences.

USPC Standards of Proficiency

The USPC has established a program of instruction and a means of testing its members. There are currently four Ratings: D, C, B, and A. The D Rating has 3 levels; the C Rating has 3 levels; the B Rating has 1 level; the A Rating has 2 levels.

The *D Ratings* are an introduction to the fun and challenge of riding and are designed to establish the foundation for safe habits and a good knowledge of the daily care of the pony and tack.

The *C Ratings* teach the Pony Clubber to become an active horseperson, to care independently for his or her pony and tack, and to understand the reason for what he or she is doing.

Pony Club Information

To find out the name and location of the Pony Club nearest you and for more information about the Pony Club, contact The United States Pony Clubs, Inc., The Kentucky Horse Park, 4071 Iron Works Pike, Lexington, KY 40511. (606) 254-7669.

The *B Rating* is for the member who wants to gain proficiency in all phases of riding and care. The B Rated member should be able to ride and care for another person's experienced horse without undoing any of the horse's education. The B member is able to clearly explain the reasons for what he or she is doing and contributes to the education of the younger Pony Clubbers.

The *A Rating* is divided into two parts, H-A and A. The H-A covers horse management, teaching, and training. The A tests the member's riding skills. The H-A rated Pony Clubber has the ability to evaluate and care for a horse's needs in a variety of circumstances and is able to teach riding and horse care to others. The A is able to ride horses at various levels of training and is able to train young horses and retrain spoiled horses.

Future Farmers of America

The Future Farmers of America (FFA), organized in 1928, has over 400,000 members who participate in programs related to agriculture. The FFA is dedicated to helping young people develop their potential for premier leadership, personal growth, and career success through agriculture education.

You must be in at least 10th grade to become an FFA member. There is an FFA Agricultural Proficiency Award Program to help members develop their interest in a particular agricultural subject. The Horse Proficiency Program gives members an idea of what is involved in breeding and raising horses. It can also involve experience programs that may result in career opportunities in the horse business.

Types of Horse Shows

You can demonstrate your horsemanship at different types of horse shows.

FFA Motto

Learning to Do
Doing to Learn
Earning to Live
Living to Serve

FFA Information

For more information on FFA, write to P.O. Box 15160, Alexandria, VA 22309, or call (703) 360-3600.

Schooling Show

A schooling show is a practice show that is usually held before the regular show season begins. Sometimes you can dress more casually for a schooling show than you can for a formal horse show. Sometimes you can use training tack. And if it is in the winter, it is okay if your horse is very fuzzy.

Breed Show

A breed show is a show that is only for registered horses of a certain breed. For example, an AQHA (American Quarter Horse Association) show is only for horses that are registered with the AQHA.

Youth Show

A youth show is a show for riders 18 years and under.

Open Show

An open show is a show that is open to all ages and breeds of horses and all ages of riders.

Horse Show Organizations

American Horse Shows Association (AHSA)

AHSA Information

For more information about the AHSA and its programs, contact AHSA at 220 East 42nd Street, New York, NY 10017, or phone (212) 972-2472.

The AHSA was founded in 1917 and serves to regulate competitions for many breed and discipline groups. A discipline is a particular style of horse use such as dressage, jumping, driving, Western riding, and hunter classes. Most of the members of AHSA participate in hunter/jumper classes, dressage, or three-day eventing.

Junior riders (those under the age of 18) can participate in many of the events at AHSA horse shows, including equitation classes, pony classes, and vaulting.

American Quarter Horse Association Youth Program

The American Quarter Horse Association (AQHA) was established in 1940 to record and preserve pedigrees of registered American Quarter Horses and to encourage members to participate in various activities with their Quarter Horses. The AQHA has 300,000 members and sponsors 2,250 shows every year.

The American Junior Quarter Horse Association (AJQHA) is designed for members under 18 years of age. An AJQHA show is usually held in conjunction with a regular AQHA show. There are 23 youth-only events including Western, English, showmanship, and halter classes. If you are new to showing, you can compete in special classes for beginning horsemen. These classes are in the Novice Youth Division. The AJQHA has a World Show in which individuals and teams from around the world compete.

There is usually at least one AJQHA youth club in each state. The purpose of the local clubs is to allow members to meet people, gain confidence, and learn how AQHA works. Members can participate in public speaking contests, horse judging contests, marketing contests, and apply for scholarships and awards.

The AQHA has a Horseback Riding Program for members who enjoy trail riding. After you join, you keep a log of the number of hours spent riding your American Quarter Horse and when you accumulate 50 hours, you receive a special award. You can continue earning awards for 100, 250, 500, 1000, 2000, and 3000 hours as well. Awards are patches, belt buckles, and gift certificates.

Other Associations with Youth Programs

There are many other breed and performance associations with youth programs. I suggest you write to the American Horse Council and purchase a Horse

AQHA Information

For more information on the AQHA and its programs, write to AQHA, P.O. Box 200, Amarillo, Texas 79168.

Horse Industry Directory

American Horse Council, 1700 K Street, NW, Suite 300, Washington, DC 20006. Phone (202) 296-4031.

Industry Directory. This big 150-page book lists the names and addresses of all horse organizations in the United States.

In the Horse Industry Directory, you'll find the addresses of the following associations that have youth classes or programs:

- American Morgan Horse Association (AMHA)
- American Paint Horse Association (APHA)
- Appaloosa Horse Club (ApHC)
- International Arabian Horse Association (IAHA)
- International Buckskin Horse Association (IBHA)
- National Cutting Horse Association (NCHA)
- National Reining Horse Association (NRHA)
- North American Trail Ride Conference (NATRC)
- Palomino Horse Breeders Association (PHBA)
- Pony of the Americas (POA)
- United States Combined Training Association (USCTA)
- United States Dressage Federation (USDF)
- and many, many others

Horse Care Calendar

Mid-Winter

■ Be sure your horse is drinking plenty of water during the cold weather.

■ Monitor his weight (see Late Summer).

Late Winter

■ Deworm for all worms and bots.

Early Spring

■ Spring dental check up.

■ This is usually a wet period so be sure your horse's hooves stay clean and dry.

■ Take horses off winter pasture so they don't tear up the soft earth with their hooves.

■ Let the pasture grasses grow.

Mid-Spring

■ Check for ticks.

■ Deworm for all worms and bots.

■ Vaccinate for at least sleeping sickness, tetanus, influenza, and rhinopneumonitis. Maybe for strangles, rabies, and other diseases (ask your vet).

- Mares start coming into heat.

- Spring conditioning program underway or begin.

- Gradually start feeding your horse some grain according to the amount of work he will be doing.

- Keep an eye on pastures for the appearance of poisonous weeds.

- Shedding begins.

Late Spring

- Check your fences and gates and make repairs.

- May begin introducing your horse gradually to spring pasture.

- Be sure your horse has free-choice salt and minerals in stalls, pens, and pastures.

- Heavy shedding of winter coat and growth of new short, summer coat occurs.

Early Summer

- Deworm for all worms.

- Rotate pastures.

- Provide shelter from the summer sun.

Mid-Summer

- Rotate pasture.

- Consider using fly sheet and fly mask.

- Check horse's weight to be sure he is not getting too fat from summer pasture.

- Buy your year's supply of hay.

Late Summer

■ Deworm for all worms.

■ Rotate pasture.

■ Shedding of summer coat and the beginning of the growth of long, winter coat.

■ Use a weight tape and feel your horse's ribs once a month from now until spring. You won't be able to tell if your horse is getting too thin by just looking at him because his fuzzy winter coat might make him look fatter than he really is.

Early Fall

■ Rotate pastures.

■ Remove bot eggs.

■ Perhaps begin blanketing at night.

■ Fall dental check-up and maybe some Rhino and Influenza booster shots.

■ If you live where there is winter cold, allow your horse to gain 5 percent but not more than 10 percent of his body weight. A 1200-pound adult horse could gain 60–120 pounds in the early fall. This extra flesh and fat will provide added insulation and an energy and heat reserve when weather is particularly bad.

■ Take horses off winter pasture before they have eaten it down.

■ Check your fences and make repairs.

Mid-Fall

■ Deworm for worms and bots after the first hard frost.

- Remove bot eggs.

- Mares stop coming into heat.

- You might need your horseshoer to put winter shoes on your horse.

Late Fall

- For every ten degrees Fahrenheit below freezing (32°F), increase hay portion of ration by 10 percent. When it is 12°F (that is, twenty degrees below freezing), the hay ration should be increased 20 percent. If a 1200-pound horse usually gets 18 pounds per day (using the usual recommendation of about 1.5 percent of the body weight as a base) then when his ration is increased 20 percent, he would get 21.6 pounds of hay per day. (Here is how you figure: 18 pounds x 20 percent = 3.6 additional pounds. Add this to his original 18 pounds and you get 21.6 pounds.) Horses that are fed less than they need to combat cold and wind will burn fat and muscle tissue by shivering to keep warm so they will lose weight and be even colder.

- Decrease the horse's grain if his activity level is low.

- Be sure he has good shelter from the snow, wet, cold, and wind.

- You can start turning your horse back on pasture once there is a blanket of snow covering it.

Early Winter

- Deworm for all worms.

REMEMBER!

- **Every day** your horse should have a daily inspection which includes his hooves.

- **Every 6–8 weeks** he should have professional farrier care, either trimming or shoeing.

Recommended Reading

Judy Chapple, *Your Horse: A Step-by-Step Guide to Horse Ownership* (North Adams, MA: Storey Publishing, 1984).

Gail Damerow, *Fences for Pasture & Garden* (North Adams, MA: Storey Publishing, 1992).

Jan Dawson, *Teaching Safe Horsemanship: A Guide to English & Western Instruction.* (North Adams, MA: Storey Publishing, 1997, 2003).

Lucinda Green, *The Young Rider* (New York, NY: Dorling Kindersley, 1993).

Jessie Haas, *Safe Horse, Safe Rider: A Young Rider's Guide to Responsible Horsekeeping* (North Adams, MA: Storey Publishing, 1994).

Susan Harris, *Grooming to Win* (New York, NY: Macmillan, 1991).

Susan Harris, *The United States Pony Club Manual of Horsemanship* (New York, NY: Macmillan, 1994).

N. Bruce Haynes, DVM, *Keeping Livestock Healthy: A Veterinary Guide to Horses, Cattle, Pigs, Goats & Sheep* (North Adams, MA: Storey Publishing, 1994).

Mary Ashby McDonald, *Starting & Running Your Own Horse Business* (North Adams, MA: Storey Publishing, 1997).

Cherry Hill, *Becoming an Effective Rider: Developing Your Mind and Body for Balance and Unity* (North Adams, MA: Storey Publishing, 1991).

Cherry Hill, *From the Center of the Ring: An Inside View of Horse Competition* (North Adams, MA: Storey Publishing, 1988).

Cherry Hill, *Horse for Sale; How to Buy a Horse or Sell the One You Have* (New York, NY: Macmillan, 1995).

Cherry Hill, *Horse Handling & Grooming: A Step-by-Step Photographic Guide* (North Adams, MA: Storey Publishing, 1997).

Cherry Hill, *Horse Health Care: A Step-by-Step Photographic Guide* (North Adams, MA: Storey Publishing, 1997).

Cherry Hill, *Horsekeeping on a Small Acreage: Facilities Design and Management* (North Adams, MA: Storey Publishing, 1990).

Cherry Hill, *101 Arena Exercises: A Ringside Guide for Horse & Rider* (North Adams, MA: Storey Publishing, 1995).

Cherry Hill and Richard Klimesh, *Maximum Hoof Power: How to Improve Your Horse's Performance Through Proper Hoof Management* (New York, NY: Macmillan, 1994).

Jane Kidd, *Learning to Ride* (New York, NY: Howell Book House, 1992).

Lon Lewis, *Feeding and Care of the Horse* (Philadelphia, PA: Williams & Wilkins, 1995).

John J. Mettler Jr., DVM, *Horse Sense: A Complete Guide to Horse Selection & Care* (North Adams, MA: Storey Publishing, 1989).

These and other books from Storey Publishing are available wherever quality books are sold or by calling 1-800-441-5700. Visit us at www.storey.com.

Glossary

action (n.). The degree of flexion of the joints of the legs during movement; also reflected in head, neck, and tail carriage. High, snappy action is desired in some classes while easy, ground-covering action is the goal in other classes.

age (of the horse) (n.). Computed from January 1 of the year in which the horse is foaled.

aid (n.). An aid is an action by a part of the rider's or handler's body to a part of the horse's body to cause the horse to react in a particular way. An aid is almost never used alone but always used in conjunction with other aids. A rider's natural aids are his or her mind, seat, weight, upper body, legs, hands, and voice. The combined use of all of the rider's aids simultaneously produce a smooth, balanced response from a horse. A handler's natural aids are the mind, hands, and overall body language. Examples of Artificial Aids (which are extensions, reinforcements, or substitutions for the natural aids) are whips, spurs, and nosebands.

appointments (n.). Tack and equipment (attire is sometimes included).

attire (n.). The rider's clothes.

back (n. and v.). A two-beat diagonal gait in reverse.

bad habit (n.). Undesirable behavior during training or handling. Examples are rearing, halter pulling, striking.

balance (n.). In regard to conformation, desirable proportions.

balk (v.). To refuse or cease to move forward.

barn sour (adj.). Herd-bound; a bad habit that may result in a horse bolting back to the barn or to his herd-mates.

bay (n. and adj.). A body color ranging from tan to reddish-brown, with black mane and tail, and usually black on the lower legs.

beat (n.). A single step in a gait, involving one leg or two. For example, the walk is a 4-beat gait, with each beat stepped off by a single leg, one at a time, 1-2-3-4. The trot is a 2-beat gait, stepped off by two legs landing at the same time, 1-2.

biting (n.). A bad habit common to young horses, stallions, and spoiled horses. It can result from hand-fed treats, petting, or improper training.

black (adj. or n.). A body color that is true black over the entire body, but may have white leg and face markings.

blemish (n.). A visible defect that does not affect serviceability.

bloodlines (n.). The family lineage.

blue roan (n. and adj.). A body color that has a uniform mixture of black and white hairs all over the body.

bolt (v.). Gulp feed without chewing; run away with rider.

bot block (n.). A rough, porous "stone" used to scrub off bot eggs.

bot fly (n.). A fly that looks like a bee and lays eggs in a horse's hair.

bowed tendon (n.). The damage to a tendon usually caused by overstretching due to improper conditioning, overwork, or an accident.

breed character (n.). The quality of conforming to the description of a particular breed.

breed registry (n.). An organization that keeps track of all the ancestors and current members of a breed.

broodmare (n.). A mare used for breeding.

brown (adj. and n.). A body color with mixed brown and black hair, with black mane, tail, and legs.

buckskin (adj. and n.). A body color that is tan, yellow, or gold with black mane, tail, and lower legs.

canter (n. and v.). The English term for a three-beat gait with right and left leads. The canter has the same foot fall pattern as the lope.

chestnut (n. and adj.). A color in which the body, mane, and tail are various shades of brown.

cob (n.). A small horse.

Coggins test (n.). A laboratory blood test used to detect previous exposure to equine infectious anemia.

cold-blooded (adj.). Refers to horses having ancestors that trace to heavy war horses and draft breeds. Characteristics might include more substance of bone, thick skin, heavy hair coat, shaggy fetlocks, and blood that makes it suitable for slow, hard work.

colic (n.). Intestinal discomfort, which can range from a mild stomachache to a life-threatening violent frenzy.

color (n.). Description of body coat color and pattern.

colt (n.). A young male horse to age four.

conditioning (n.). The art and science of preparing a horse mentally and physically for a particular use such as pleasure riding, competitive trail riding, or showing.

conformation (n.). The physical structure of a horse, which is compared to a standard of perfection or an ideal.

cribbing (n. and v.). A vice whereby a horse anchors its teeth onto an object, arches its neck, pulls backward, and swallows air. It can cause the horse to lose weight, suffer tooth damage, and other physical disturbances. It can be a contagious habit.

crossbred (n. and adj.). A horse that has one parent of one breed and the other parent of another breed.

cross-tie (n. and v.). A means of tying a horse in which a chain or rope from each side of an aisle is attached to the side rings of the horse's halter.

cryptorchidism (n.). The retention of one or both testicles in the abdominal cavity.

cue (n.). A single signal, often made up of several aids, from the rider or handler that tells a horse what to do. Often used in performing tricks.

dam (n.). Mother of a horse.

diagonal (n.). A pair of legs at the trot, such as the right front and the left hind. When posting, the rider sits as the inside hind hits the ground or "rise and fall with the (front) leg on the wall." Riding across the diagonal is a maneuver from one corner of an arena to another through the center.

disunited (adv.). Cantering or loping on different leads front and hind.

dock (n.). The flesh and bone portion of the tail.

draft horse (n.). A horse of one of the breeds of "heavy horses" developed for farm or freight work, such as Percheron, Belgian, and Clydesdale. Draft horses weigh 1,500–2,200 pounds and can be as tall as 17 hands. They are not suitable for riding.

driving (adj. and v.). Description of a horse or pony used to pull a wagon or cart.

dun (n. and adj.). A yellow or gold body and leg color, often with a black or brown mane and tail, and usually with a dorsal stripe and stripes on the legs and withers.

English (adj.). Referring to riding with English tack and attire.

equestrian (adj.). Of or pertaining to horsemen or horsemanship; a rider.

equitation (n.). The art of riding.

farrier (n.). A person who shoes horses.

fetlock (n.). The joint between a horse's pastern and cannon.

filly (n.). A female horse to age 4.

flank (n.). The area of a horse's barrel between the rib cage and the hindquarters.

flaxen (adj.). A golden mane or tail on a darker-bodied horse.

floating (n. and v.). The process of filing off sharp edges of a horse's teeth.

foal (n.). A male or female horse or pony under 1 year of age.

forehand (n.). That portion of the horse from the heart girth forward.

forelock (n.). The hair growing between a horse's ears that falls on the forehead; a horse's "bangs."

founder (n. and v.). Another word for laminitis, a serious disease affecting a horse's hooves and often caused by a horse's eating too much grain or green pasture.

frog (n.). The thick, triangle-shaped tissue on the bottom of a horse's hooves.

gait (n.). A specific pattern of foot movements such as the walk, trot, and canter.

gaited horse (n.). An animated horse such as the Arabian, American Saddlebred, Morgan, or Tennessee Walking Horse with flashy gaits.

gelding (n.). A male horse that has been castrated (had its testicles removed).

grade (adj. and n.). An unregistered horse.

gray (adj. and n.). A color in which the skin is black, and the hair is a mixture of black and white.

green (adj.). An inexperienced horse or rider, relatively speaking.

ground training (n.). When the trainer works the horse from the ground, rather than being mounted. Includes in-hand work, barn manners, longeing, and ground driving.

grullo (n. and adj.). A type of dun with a smoky or mouse-colored body, and usually having a black mane, tail, lower legs, and dorsal stripe.

halter class (n.). Conformation class.

halter pulling (n.). A bad habit in which a horse pulls violently backward on the halter rope when tied.

hand (n.). Horses are measured from the highest point of the withers to the ground in units called hands. One hand equals four inches. 14•2 means (14 hands x 4 inches) + 2 inches, which is 56 inches + 2 inches = 58 inches.

haunches (n.). Hindquarters.

head shy (adj.). Description of a horse who shies away from having his head touched.

heart girth (n.). The measurement taken around the horse's barrel just behind the front legs.

heat (n.). The part of a mare's reproductive cycle when she is ready to mate with a stallion.

heaves (n.). Damage to the lungs, resulting in labored breathing.

herd-bound (adj.). When a horse is too dependent on being with other horses and doesn't want to be separated from them.

honest (adj.). A quality in a horse which makes him dependable and predictable.

horse (n.). An equine over 14•2 hands.

horsemanship (n.). Exhibition of a rider's skill, usually referring to the Western style of riding.

hot-blooded (adj.). Refers to horses having ancestors that trace to Thoroughbreds or Arabians. Characteristics might include fineness of bone, thin skin, fine hair coat, absence of long fetlock hairs, and blood that makes it well-suited for speed and distance work.

hunter (n.). A type of horse, not a breed, which is suitable for field hunting or show hunting.

in-hand class (n.). A class in which the horse is led by the exhibitor.

jog (n. and v.). A slow Western trot.

junior (n.). A rider under eighteen years of age as of January 1.

larvae (n.). Insects or parasites that have hatched from eggs but are not yet mature.

lead (n.). A specific footfall pattern at the canter or lope in which the inside legs of the circle reach farther forward than the outside legs. When working to the right on the right lead, the horse's right foreleg and right hind leg reach farther forward than the left legs. If a horse is loping in a circle to the right on the left lead, he is said to be on the wrong lead or is counter-cantering.

liver chestnut (n. and adj.). A very dark red chestnut color, with mane, tail, and legs the same color as the body or flaxen.

longe (v.). To work a horse in a circle usually on a 30-foot line around you at various gaits.

lope (n. and v.). A three-beat gait: (1) an initiating hind leg; (2) a diagonal pair including the leading hind leg and the diagonal foreleg; and (3) the leading foreleg.

manners (n). The energetic yet cooperative attitude of a horse.

mare (n.). A female horse over age four.

markings (n.). White on the face or legs of a horse.

muzzle (n.). The end of a horse's face, including the nose, nostrils, and lips.

near side (n.). The horse's left side.

novice (n.). In general, an inexperienced horseperson.

off side (n.). The horse's right side.

pacing (n.). Continuous stall or pen walking. Often an unhappy horse's reaction to confinement.

paddock (n.). A small pasture.

Paint (n. and adj.). A breed of horse with large blocks of white and black or white and brown.

paint (n. and adj.). Coat pattern on any breed of horse that is similar to that on a Paint Horse.

Palomino (n. and adj.). A breed of horse that has a golden body color and a light to white mane and tail.

palomino (n. and adj.). A horse with coloring similar to that of a Palomino Horse.

panic snap (n.). A safety snap often used in horse trailers and cross-ties. The design allows the snap to be released even if there is great pressure on it.

parasite (n.). A harmful organism that lives in or on another organism.

park horse (n.). A horse with a brilliant performance, style, presence, finish, balance and cadence and usually animated gaits.

parrot mouth (n.). An unsoundness of the teeth characterized by an extreme overbite.

pattern (n.). A prescribed order of maneuvers in a particular class such as reining or trail.

pawing (n.). A bad habit usually caused by nervousness and/or improper ground training; can also be a sign of colic.

pecking order (n.). Social rank of each horse in a group; one horse is the boss and the others find their place.

pedigree (n.). A listing of a horse's ancestors.

pen (n.). An outdoor living space that is at least 24 feet long and 24 feet wide.

points (n.). The coloring of the legs, mane, and tail.

poll (n.). The junction of the vertebrae with the skull located between a horse's ears; an area of great sensitivity and flexion.

pony (n.). A horse that stands 58 inches (14•2 hands) or less.

posting (n.). A way to ride the English trot; see *diagonal*.

presence (n.). Personality, charisma.

pulse (n.). Heart rate. Normal adult resting heart rate varies among horses but is usually 40 beats per minute.

pupae (n.). The stage of development between the bot egg and the bot fly.

purebred (n. and adj.). A horse of pure ancestors of a particular breed.

quality (n.). Overall degree of merit: flat bone and clean joints, refined features and fine skin and hair coat.

rearing (n.). A bad habit in a horse, of raising up on his hind legs when he is being led or ridden. An extremely dangerous habit that should be dealt with by a professional only.

red roan (n. and adj.). A mixture of red and white hairs all over a horse's body, with red, black, or flaxen mane and tail. Also called *strawberry roan*.

refinement (n.). Quality appearance, indicating good breeding.

registered (adj.). A horse of purebred parents that have numbered certificates with a particular breed organization.

rein-back (n.). To back up; a two-beat diagonal gait in reverse.

respiration rate (n.). Number of breaths per minute. Normal adult respiration rate varies among horses but is usually 12 to 15 breaths per minute. One breath consists of an inhalation and an exhalation.

ringbone (n.). An arthritic unsoundness of the pastern joint.

ring sour (adj.). A poor attitude in a horse who does not enjoy working in an arena and looks for ways to leave the arena or quit working.

roached (adj.). A mane or tail that has been clipped to the skin.

roan (n. and adj.). A horse color resulting from a mixture of white and black or white and red hairs all over the body.

roaring (n.). A breathing disorder.

run (n.). A long, narrow fenced-in area usually attached to a stall.

sand colic (n.). A digestive disorder that occurs when a horse eats sand or dirt with his feed.

sheath (n.). The skin folds that encase a horse's penis.

showmanship (n.). An in-hand class that is judged on the exhibitor's ability to show his horse.

shying (n.). A horse spooking or becoming startled by a movement or object. It may or may not include a sudden jump sideways, or bolting.

sire (n.). Father of a horse.

sorrel (n. and adj.). A reddish or copper-red body with mane and tail the same color as the body.

sound (adj.). Having no defect, visible or unseen, that affects serviceability; the state of being able to perform without hindrance.

spavin (n.). An unsoundness of the hock which can involve soft tissues (bog spavin) or bone (bone spavin or jack spavin).

spayed mare (n.). A neutered female horse.

splint boots (n.). Protective covering worn around the cannons of the front legs to prevent injury.

splints (n.). A term referring to bony enlargements at various points along either of the splint bones, located on each side of the cannon bone.

spooky (adj.). An easily startled horse.

sport horse (n.). A purebred or crossbred horse suitable for dressage, jumping, eventing, or endurance.

stallion (n.). A male horse (not gelded).

step (n.). A beat.

stock horse (n.). A Western-style horse of the Quarter Horse type.

strawberry roan (n. and adj.). A mixture of red and white hairs all over a horse's body, with red, black, or flaxen mane and tail. Also called *red roan.*

stride (n.). The distance traveled in a particular gait, measured from the spot where one hoof hits the ground to where it next lands. Ten to twelve feet is the normal length of stride at a canter, for example.

striking (n.). A bad habit of reaching out with a front foot so as to hit the handler, equipment, or another horse. A problem calling for professional help.

stud (n.). A stallion used for breeding.

substance (n.). Strength and density of bone, muscle, and tendons or an indication of large body size.

suckling (n.). A foal that is still with its mother; it has not been weaned; usually it is under four months of age.

suitability (n.). Appropriateness for a particular purpose and/or a type or size of rider.

sullen (adj.). Sulky, resentful, withdrawn.

tack (n.). Horse equipment or gear.

tail rubbing (n.). A habit that may originate from anal or skin itch or a dirty sheath or udder. Even when the cause is removed, the habit often persists.

temperament (n.). The general consistency with which a horse behaves.

temperature (n.). Normal adult temperature varies among horses, but will usually range in degrees from 99.5°F to 100.5°F.

Thoroughbred (n.). The breed of horse registered with the Jockey Club. Not meant to be used as a synonym for purebred.

thrush (n.). A disease of the hoof often associated with unsanitary conditions, which causes decomposition of the frog and other hoof structures.

topline (n.). The proportion and curvature of the outline of a horse's neck, back, and croup; a line from poll to tail-head.

tractable (adj.). A quality in a horse's disposition that makes him cooperative and trainable.

travel (n.). The path of the flight of each limb during movement.

trot (n. and v.). A two-beat diagonal gait.

twitch (n.). A means of restraint. A nose twitch is often a wooden handle with a loop of chain, applied to the horse's upper lip.

tying up (n.). A form of metabolic muscle stiffness caused from irregularity in feed and work schedules.

type (n.). A particular style of horse with certain characteristics that contribute to its value and efficiency for a particular use.

udder (n.). The mammary glands or teats of a female horse.

underline (n.). The length and shape of the line from the elbow to the sheath or udder.

unsoundness (n.). A defect that may or may not be seen but that does affect serviceability.

vice (n.). Abnormal behavior in the stable environment that results from confinement or improper management and can affect a horse's usefulness, dependability, and health. Examples are cribbing and weaving.

walk (n. and v.). A four-beat flat-footed gait.

weanling (n.). A foal that has been separated from its mother; usually 4–12 months of age.

weaving (n.). Rhythmic swaying of weight from one front foot to the other when confined. Can be socially contagious.

Western (adj.). Referring to riding with Western tack and attire.

withers (n.). The part of the horse's spine where the neck joins the back.

wood chewing (n.). A common vice that damages facilities and can cause abnormal wear of teeth and possible complications from wood splinters.

yearling (n.). A male or female horse or pony that is one year old.

youth (n. and adj.). An exhibitor eighteen years of age and under. Additional age divisions are often created to separate children further.

INDEX

Page references in *italics* indicate illustrations.